Series / Number 90-003

Traditional Patrimonialism and Modern Neopatrimonialism

S. N. EISENSTADT

The Hebrew University of Jerusalem

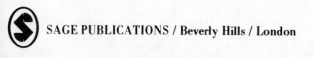

SAGE PUBLICATIONS / Beverly Hills / London

For information address:

SAGE PUBLICATIONS, INC.
275 South Beverly Drive
Beverly Hills, California 90212

SAGE PUBLICATIONS, INC.
St George's House / 44 Hatton Garden
London EC1N 8ER

International Standard Book Number 0-8039-0371-5

Library of Congress Catalog Card No. L.C. 73-89066

FIRST PRINTING

When citing a Research Paper, please use the proper form. Remember to cite the series title and include the paper number. One of the two following formats can be adapted (depending on the style manual used):

(1) WEINTRAUB, D. (1973) "Development and Modernization in the Philippines: The Problem of Change in the Context of Political Stability and Social Continuity." Sage Research Papers in the Social Sciences (Studies in Comparative Modernization Series, No. 90-001). Beverly Hills and London: Sage Publications.

or

(2) Weintraub, Dov. 1973. *Development and Modernization in the Philippines: The Problem of Change in the Context of Political Stability and Social Continuity.* Sage Research Papers in the Social Sciences, vol. 1, series no. 90-001 (Studies in Comparative Modernization Series). Beverly Hills and London: Sage Publications.

Contents

Editors' Introduction to the Series *5*

I.   Introduction: The Problems of Modern Patrimonial Regimes *7*

II. Neopatrimonial Regimes *13*

The Major Aspects of Political Structure and Process in
Neopatrimonial Regimes *13*

Conditions and Foci of Cleavages and Crises in Neopatrimonial
Regimes *19*

Varieties of Neopatrimonial Regimes and the Nature of Policies
Aiming to Assure their Stability *25*

III. Traditional Patrimonial Regimes *30*

The Political Format of Traditional Patrimonial Regimes *30*

The Variety of Traditional Patrimonial Regimes *37*

IV. Conditions of Development and Continuity of Traditional and
Modern Patrimonial Regimes *40*

V.   The Dynamics of Neopatrimonial Regimes *50*

VI. Summary and Theoretical Conclusions *59*

Notes *69*

Bibliography *82*

Editor's Introduction to the Series

This series of comparative studies on modernization stems from a broad programme of research developed over the past five years in the Harry S Truman Research Institute, in cooperation with the Department of Sociology of the Hebrew University of Jerusalem, and with other departments of the Faculty of Social Sciences. Its focus is analytical and comparative—i.e., the analysis of the *diverse* social, economical and political patterns which develop in different modernizing societies and the factors which can explain such diversity.

Even though this series of papers shows considerable differences in points of view, nevertheless they have some strong common grounds; mainly, in their revision of 'classical' theories of modernization. These theories assumed that there existed a total dichotomy between 'traditional' and 'modern' societies, and that the best way for a society to modernize was to shed most of its traditional qualities.

However, the present studies support the view that the variability of modernization is not due to one factor (the traditionality of a society, or its level of development) but to a variety of factors. Neither do their authors assume that there is necessarily any negative relationship between tradition and modernity. Rather, different aspects of 'tradition' will have varying impact on the process of development, so that each society may create its own version of modernity.

So we may say of much of this research that it:

First, recognizes what may be called the systemic viability of the so-called transitional systems;

Second, assumes these societies may develop in ways not necessarily envisioned by the initial model of modernization;

Third, they recognize the importance of both the different aspects of historical continuity and of the international situation for shaping differing contours of development for different contemporary 'post-traditional' social orders.

5

The crystallization of any post-traditional society is influenced by a combination of social factors, including:

- The level of resources available for mobilization and institution-building,
- The manner in which the forces of modernity impinge on the particular society,
- The structure of the situation of change in which they are caught, and,
- The different traditions of these societies or civilizations as embodied in their 'pre-modern' socio-economic structure.

Differing combinations of these forces will influence different aspects of the contours and dynamics of the post-traditional socio-political order; each individual force will tend to have more influence on some developmental aspects than on others.

The studies which will be published in this series will test these generalizations against specific case studies, or in comparative analyses.

—S. N. EISENSTADT

Editors' Note:
The editors would like to express their gratitude to the Founders and Overseers of the Harry S Truman Research Institute for their support and assistance in the development of this series.
                                                                —S.N.E. and D.W.

TRADITIONAL PATRIMONIALISM AND MODERN NEOPATRIMONIALISM

S . N. EISENSTADT

Professor of Sociology, The Hebrew University, Jerusalem

I. INTRODUCTION: THE PROBLEMS OF MODERN PATRIMONIAL REGIMES

In recent literature on developing societies and on New Nations there has been a growing tendency to describe the political regimes of a large part of these societies in terms which were usually used to describe various traditional political systems.

G. Roth and A. Zolberg were probably among the first scholars to use the term of patrimonial in this context—Zolberg applying it to many of the African States while G. Roth gave it a wider connotation.[1] In a somewhat similar vein Gellner and Waterbury, in some recent works on North Africa,[2] have emphasized that the contemporary political regimes of pre-colonial Maghreb can perhaps be best understood in such terms which have also been characteristic of the traditional regimes in these regions.

To some (but only to some) degree, they follow Geertz's earlier analysis, in which he analyzed contemporary Indonesian politics in terms of the traditional Javanese 'theatre state'[3] as well as Riggs' attempts to analyze some of these regimes in terms of the 'sala' model.[4]

Among all these terms the connotation 'patrimonial,' derived as it was from a relatively long tradition of sociological and political analysis

AUTHOR'S NOTE: This paper constitutes an elaboration of several presentations given at the interdepartmental seminar on Comparative Problems of Modernization and Tradition. The seminar was given at the Faculty of Social Sciences (The Eliezer Kaplan School of Economics and Social Sciences) and the Department of Sociology of the Hebrew University. I am greatly indebted to Mrs. Yael Atzmon, Mrs. Yael Levi, Dr. N. Levtzion and Dr. M. Rudner and to the students participating in the seminar for their continuous discussions. The research on which this paper is based has been supported by the Truman Research Center of the Hebrew University and the Units of Modernization at the Eliezer Kaplan School of Economics and Social Sciences.

most fully epitomized in Weber's work, has been the most general and 'systematic.'

The connotation of these regimes as 'patrimonial' or the like was not merely descriptive. In Roth's, as well as to some degree in Zolberg's analysis, the use of the term patrimonial explicitly constituted a critical attitude to some of the basic assumptions of the first studies of modernization and political development; to the first attempts at overcoming the difficulties with which these assumptions were confronted in face of the continuously changing reality of these countries; and in face of diversification of research findings in these fields.

Among the more important of these assumptions were, first, that the conditions for sustained growth, for continuous development and modernization in different institutional fields are dependent upon or tantamount to, continuous extension of these various sociodemographic and/or structural indices of modernization. According to this view, the more a society exhibits or develops the basic characteristics of structural specialization and the more developed it is on various indices of social mobilization, the less traditional and the more modern it would be; i.e., by implication, the better it would be able to develop continuously, to deal continuously with new problems and social forces and to develop a continuously expanding institutional structure.

Closely related to these assumptions was the implicit vision of the end-product of modernization or of political development in terms of the Western ideal of a 'nation-state'; or a revolutionary class-society, i.e., of a political order characterized by: (a) a high degree of congruence between the cultural and the political identities of the territorial population; (b) a high level of symbolic and affective commitments to the social and cultural centers and a close relation between these centers and the more primordial dimensions of human existence; (c) a marked emphasis on common politically defined collective goals for all members of the national community; and (d) by a continuous tension between a transcendental ideal of social order and the actual reality.

By the 1950s and early 1960s it had become apparent that these assumptions could not hold;[5] that the various sociodemographic or structural indices of modernization indicate only the extent to which traditional, self-contained societies or communities became weakened, or disintegrated, or to paraphrase the title of Dan Lerner's book—the extent to which Transitional Society is Passing. But they do not in themselves indicate the extent to which a new, viable, modern (or post-traditional) society which is capable of continuous growth, may develop or exactly what kind of society will develop and what its exact institutional contours will be.

Similarly, it became clear that the mere destruction of traditional forms of life does not necessarily assure the development of such a new, viable, modern society, and that very often the disruption of traditional settings, 'be they family, community, or even political', tends to lead more to disorganization, delinquency and chaos rather than to the foundation of a new viable modern order.

There was also a continuously growing awareness of the historical facts that in many countries modernization has been successfully implemented under the aegis of traditional symbols—and even by traditional elites. In such countries as Japan, and even in England, many traditional symbols—be they the Emperor of Japan, the traditional symbols of the realm in Britain, or the traditional symbols of provincial life in Holland—were retained or even reinforced. In many other cases, as for instance in Russia, when the modernizing elites attempted to undermine such traditional symbols, there soon followed an attempt, even if in a halting way, to revive them.

The early recognition of the inadequacy of many of the assumptions of the initial studies of modernization for the analysis of many New Nations has given rise to the concepts of 'breakdowns' of modernization and of 'political decay'[6]; to the analysis of the conditions under which such breakdowns and political decay take place in these societies, and the emergence of the concept of 'traditional' societies as a key concept in the studies of modernization.[7]

But even these concepts and analyses were yet largely bound by some of the premises of the earlier models of modernization—as can be seen, for instance, in the fact that these analyses have not asked what may happen after such 'breakdowns,' or what type of sociopolitical orders could develop after such periods of decay or breakdowns. It seems that these analyses somehow assumed—even if only implicitly—that after such a breakdown there will take place either a new recuperation towards some modernity, or a general regression towards some (unspecified) chaotic instability. They assumed also that those 'transitional' societies which will not ultimately break down, will move in the direction of the ultimate common, universal end plateau of modernity.

But while, truly enough, the elements of such chaos and institutional instability were not lacking—whether in Africa or Burma, in Indonesia or Latin America—this very instability tended often to evince some continuous and systematic pattern of its own. Such breakdowns or stagnation did not necessarily lead to the total collapse of these new regimes or to their return to some traditional social and political form. These polities certainly differ in many ways from the 'older' (Western) modern ones, and they do not necessarily develop in the direction of other (Russian or Javanese) models of modernity. Yet, however strong their similarity to their traditional settings, they are by no means any longer simple replications of these settings. Moreover, however stagnant or unstable these regimes may seem to be, they evince some capability of reorganization and continuity and they develop various internal and external policies which aim at assuring for themselves the conditions of such continuity.

The use of the term 'patrimonial' in the depicting of these various regimes implied, as indicated above, a reaction to the inadequacies of the central assumptions of the basic studies of modernization, as well as the later concepts such as 'breakdown,' 'political decay' or 'transitional' societies. It emphasized the inadequacy of these assumptions by indicating first, that many of these societies and states did not develop into the direction of some modern nation-states or revolutionary societies; second, that these regimes did not necessarily constitute a 'transitory,' 'transitional,' passing phase towards an inevitable path to one type of modernity; third, by indicating that there was yet some internal 'logic' in their development; and, last, by emphasizing that part at least of this logic or pattern could be derived from some aspects of the traditions of these societies and understood in terms of these aspects.

The various post-traditional societies—to which the term patrimonialism has been applied lately—were mostly among the latecomers to modernization; they comprised especially Southeast Asia, Southern Indonesia, Malaysia, Ceylon, Burma, most Latin American societies and many of the Middle Eastern ones.

Initially these societies were presented with several different models of modernity, i.e., with models of how to cope with these problems and how to organize and shape their new, nontraditional social and political orders. Of these, two are of special importance: first, the ideological model, and second, the actual model of colonial rule in Asia and Africa and the model that developed in Latin America through the impact of the former Spanish Empire.

The ideological model—presented mostly by various Western intellectuals and very often taken up by the first generations of intellectuals within those societies—was that of the European nation-state and 'class society'—whether in the 'liberal,' 'national' or later on the socialist and communist terms.

At the same time, however, the initial institutional framework into which these societies were put was that of colonial or semi-colonial (i.e., trusteeship, etc.) regimes in which elements of two different models interacted.[8] Side by side with important elements related to nation-state model, such as territorial unification, universalistic administration and legal principles and claims—however weak or hypocritical—to some transcendental legitimation, there prevailed in such colonial regimes also rather important elements which were closer to those found in patrimonial regimes. The most important among these have been the largely adaptive relations between the center and periphery and the lack of congruency between the boundaries of the political, ethnic and cultural units and communities.

During the struggle for independence and immediately after its attainment the elites of many of these societies have seemingly indeed adopted the 'nation-state' or 'class-revolutionary' model and have attempted to shape the contours of their new societies accordingly. However, as we have seen above, the later developments of these societies did not, in most cases, go in the direction of these models. It was indeed, as we have seen, the lack of ability to institutionalize such models that was often described in terms of 'breakdown of modernization' or of 'political decay' —and later on gave rise to the description of these regimes as patrimonial.

But the definition or description of these regimes as 'patrimonial' poses some obvious difficulties or problems. The term 'patrimonialism' as applied to political regimes—and not only as a purely accidental or marginal phenomenon of political life—has usually been used to describe relatively noncomplex, nondifferentiated historical, traditional, political regimes.[9]

How can it then be meaningfully—and not only metaphorically— applied to much more complex contemporary types of political regimes characterized by such organizational forms of political life as bureaucracies, parties of popular movements—however weak they may be—which clearly are beyond the scope of relatively noncomplex and traditional polities?

Truly enough in the recent application of the term 'patrimonialism' to these regimes one aspect of patrimonialism—mainly its personalism and the attempts of their personalistic rulers to perpetuate themselves in positions of power—have been singled out and have been used to explain the low level of stability of such regimes.[10] But such personalistic aspects of these regimes are not enough to explain the dynamics of these regimes, their more continuous features, the conditions of their development, continuity and change.

Indeed, such emphasis on pure personalism and instability is to some degree akin to the terminology of 'breakdown' and 'decay' referred to earlier, against which, as we have seen, the very use of the term patrimonial in the study of new states was intended.

The purely personalistic aspect of these regimes does not explain the fact that many of them have evinced—in the very changes and oscillations which characterize them, when compared to nation-state models, as epitomes of instability—a certain continuing pattern which in many ways may be similar to that which can be found in the less differentiated, traditional societies which have been denoted as patrimonial.

And indeed, the term patrimonialism—as applied both to traditional and post-traditional regimes—has in fact contained at least two additional connotations, even though the distinction between these connotations and between them and the personalistic aspects of such regimes were always fully recognized or developed.

The first such additional connotation—to be found among the modern scholars in the writings of Roth, and to some degree also in the writings of Zolberg—tends to stress that these patrimonial regimes are less differentiated, less complex than the more routinized and organized ones, such as nation-state and revolutionary models in the contemporary 'modern' world, or the Imperial regimes among traditional polities.

The second connotation, brought out to some degree also by these scholars but more fully by Gellner, Waterbury and Geertz, stresses not so much the degree of stability or complexity of these systems, but rather certain 'modes' of coping with political problems.[11]

Some such distinction between these different aspects of patrimonialism can be found already in Weber and in the writings of some of the earlier scholars who used the term with respect to traditional polities—even though the fact that this connotation was derived from a kinship-familial setting has probably made the recognition of distinction between these various aspects rather difficult.

But it is indeed the fact that the term patrimonialism comprises these various components that may provide the clues to the usefulness of the patrimonial 'model' to explain some of the major characteristics of 'traditional' and 'post-traditional' or modern regimes alike.

The very fact that already in the loci classici of definition of patrimonialism in Weber's works as well as the various attempts to apply this term in broader comparative analysis, the term 'patrimonialism' has often been applied to societies with different degrees of structural differentiation —such as tribal federations, nomad Empires, and, in Weber's parlance at least, to more unified and compact Empires—attests to the possibility of a meaningful use of the term patrimonialism in application to both non-complex and complex, traditional and possibly also to modern regimes alike. But all these analyses indicate also that such usefulness is greatest insofar as 'patrimonialism' is used to point out certain modes of coping with problems of political life and organization, which may, in principle, cut across different levels of social complexity, structural differentiation or types of regimes.

II. NEOPATRIMONIAL REGIMES

THE MAJOR ASPECTS OF POLITICAL STRUCTURE AND PROCESS IN NEOPATRIMONIAL REGIMES

The starting point of the analysis of modern 'neopatrimonial regimes' is the fact that many of these societies have developed many characteristics which differed greatly from the 'nation-state' or revolutionary models of modernity. The characteristics were not immediately apparent in the initial phases of modern development of most of these regimes; they became crystallized and 'visible' in the post-colonial societies with the dissolution or 'breakdown' of the initial models of ideological and/or institutional models of modernization, which they inherited from the colonial periods and from the period of the struggle of independence, while in many Latin American countries these patrimonial modes continued, despite the continuous attraction of other models of modernity to predominate throughout the changing social and economic conditions.

The most important such characteristics developed in the structure of the centers and of their relation to the periphery, the definition of boundaries of these societies, as well as the pattern of political organization, struggle and change within them. [12]

The first characteristic which tended to develop in these societies was a certain type of 'distinctiveness' of the center and of its relations to the periphery. This distinctiveness of the center could be seen first in the attempts of the elites to concentrate both intrasocietal power and the representation of the symbols of social and cosmic order.

There tended to develop in these societies a very strong emphasis on the representation by the political center of the 'cosmic' as well as of the social and moral order. This tendency was manifest in internal as well as external, international affairs. In the latter the growing importance of the international scene has often pushed the elites of these countries to active participation in various international events or movements, such as socialist, religious or political ('nonalignment') movements. But such participation often tended to be symbolic, striving to add to the glory of their center by the mere upholding of these symbols, but without necessarily implementing the concrete programs of these movements. Internally there tended to develop a continuously growing emphasis on concentration in the hands of the center of the custody of the moral and social order, and of the welfare of the society.

This distinctiveness could often be enhanced, insofar as the symbols and the organizational structures of the center tended to be more complex and so far as the elites and the central elites aimed to establish or maintain political entities (many of which were indeed created by the colonial powers and upheld later by the leaders of movements of independence) which were wider than those envisaged in the traditional definition of the polity or aspired to by any part of the periphery.

At the same time in most of these countries, the distinctiveness of the center did not become connected—especially after the initial and relatively unsuccessful phase of attempting to institutionalize a nation-state model of modern regime—with attempts to a structural and ideological transformation of the periphery or with effecting far-reaching changes in the periphery's basic conception of social order; in a high degree of commitment to the social order; or with the developments of new motivations for the undertaking of more differentiated roles and for developing the discipline necessary for their pursuance.

Truly enough, in most of these societies there tended seemingly to develop new types of modern, 'open,' centers. Yet this potential openness and the mutual impingement of center and periphery was here coupled with relatively little structural and symbolic permeation or transformation of the periphery by the center.

The central elites of these societies tended also to emphasize certain types of activities of the centers more than others. Thus on the one hand, they tended more and more to monopolize in their own hands the societies' external relations, the representation of the cosmic order, and to develop internally, mostly adaptive and 'extractive' administrative policies—with a very strong stress on distributive and mediatory-distributive functions. Only to a smaller degree did they tend to develop also active promotion of new intergroup relations or frameworks; to forge out symbols of a political-collective identity transcending the given social reality and which commands a high degree of commitment—all of which were basic components of the nation-state or some of the revolutionary models of modernity.

On the other hand, there took place the continuous weakening of any autonomous access by different groups and strata to the formation of the symbols of social and moral order; concomitant strengthening of the perception of the center as the sole or major repository of such, albeit 'given,' values or symbols. The conception of such order as being 'created' or 'formed' by free autonomous activities of social groups, not entirely 'given'—as was to some degree implicit in the nation-state model—tended to become dimmed and upheld more and more only by some exceptional, marginal, intellectual elites or revolutionary groups.

These tendencies in the crystallization of the centers manifested themselves in the policies developed by their elites as well as in the whole format of political organization and process that developed in these societies.

Thus in all these societies one can discern a continuous growth in the importance of what may be called paternalistic and distributive, accumulative and extractive policies.[13]

The 'paternalistic' orientations of these policies were evident in the fact that it was the center that concentrated in its hands most of the 'keys,' resources, and mechanisms necessary for development and attempted to manipulate or direct the other sectors; and concentrated in its hands the major policies of welfare and distribution.[14]

These paternalistic policies were mostly distributive, accumulative and extractive. Even when these policies were coupled with a strong developmental orientation—and even in those cases, such as Brazil, Tunisia and perhaps Peru, when this orientation was more than pure rhetoric—such developmental policies were very strongly related to distributive subsidies and tended to focus on extraction and distribution of resources; on the increase of productivity within the given institutional frameworks, rather than on the creation of new types of resources and activities either by the center or independently by the various groups in the periphery, or on the restructuring of the existing economic and social units and their interrelations.

Closely related to the preceding developments were those in the whole format of political organization and processes, in the internal structure and organization of the centers, and in the nature and channels of political struggle that developed in these societies. Here there developed a growing shift from more representative or constitutional types of political institutions, or from groups with autonomous access to the center and from independent political organization, as well as from universalistic, bureaucratic, legal and parliamentary frameworks—often inherited from the colonial period—to the executive branch of the government in general and within it to bureaucratic, army or political cliques, to pressure groups and to rather volatile populistic parties or movements.[15]

Although the compositions of such cliques or groups varied in the different societies studied here, the 'rules' of the game of any such coalition tended to emphasize the cooptation to—or exclusion from—access to the center and to the sources of distributive policies and bureaucratic positions. The 'rules' also tended to emphasize the center's mediation between such different cliques, with but little leeway for the development of autonomous access—by these or other broader groups—to such resources and positions.

Within these frameworks and patterns of coalition the major means of political struggle tended to become more and more those of cooptation, change or extension of clientele and factional networks often coupled with general populistic appeals made mostly in terms of ascriptive symbols or values representing different ethnic, religious or national communities. Such appeals could easily become upheld in outbreaks which often served as important signals for the inadequacy of the existing pattern of cooptations.

The development of such political format could manifest itself in several Middle Eastern countries, or in such countries as Burma and Indonesia, in the decline of either legislative bodies or parties and their being taken over by central bureaucratic, small personal cliques or by the army. These shifts could also take place in Malaysia, and to some degree in Ceylon, through the monopolization of power within parliamentary parties by more restricted cliques—together with the decline of the more independent groups within these parties and of independent organizations of public opinion. In Latin American countries there tended to develop, throughout their history, continuous changes and shifts between various types of oligarchic, army and bureaucratic cliques, relatively loose parties and wider populistic movements.[16]

Whatever the organizational details, these shifts in the scope and channels of political struggle denoted changes in the 'meaning' or functioning of many of those institutions—like parliaments, parties, bureaucracies and judiciary—which were taken over from the colonial or adapted from the European or North American settings and which were often initially shaped according to liberal-constitutional or other 'nation-state' models.

Parliaments tended to become additional arenas of symbolic representation of the polity, of political socialization and—especially in Latin American countries—arenas of struggle between various cliques much more than of independent representation of independent leadership of different groups and strata. Parties tended, more and more, to become instruments for the forging out of symbols of common collective identity; for regulating at least part of the access to the center and to positions controlling distributive policies, and for extensions or changes of networks of patronage rather than representing various broader, independent and/or ideological orientations.

Mobilization into parties and voting usually served the function of changing or broadening the base of access to such 'distributive' positions, of the creation of new clientele and patronage and factional networks, of access to influence on the center or of symbolizing the adherence to the symbols of polity represented by the center. But only to a lesser degree did voting or mobilization into parties serve to work out new principles of social distribution, of changing the rules of access to the center, or as attempts to influence the center from an independent basis of power according to the ideologies of such bases.

Hence, there could often develop a clash between the party and the administration or the army in competition for the performance of these functions and for the control over the central resources.

These developments gave rise to the crystallization, in these societies, of more volatile centers of power, within which the army tended to occupy a strategic position as a reservoir of actual power and as the keeper of the appropriate symbols against the corruption of other groups. This strategic position of the army was often reinforced by its very crucial role as one of the major channels of social mobility in general and into the center in particular.[17]

At the same time, especially with growing social mobilization and politization, there tended to develop, particularly among mobile or uprooted marginal groups which could not find access to the existing channels of power and patronage, various pockets and reservoirs of violence and insurgency.[18]

These tendencies within the central frameworks of these societies and among the central elites were reinforced by parallel ones among the large parts of the broadest strata. Perhaps most indicative of these tendencies among the broad groups of the society was their dependence upon the center in the regulation of their own internal affairs insofar as these were related to the broader society and only as a very weak development of any autonomous mechanisms of self-regulation. This can be most clearly seen in the nature of the political demands which tended to develop in these societies, and which given the spread of the basic assumptions of modernity, were continuously emerging and intensifying. These were usually demands for broadening access to the center, and much less for control of the center or for possible change of its contents and symbols, or for creation of new types of social and cultural orders.

Even in the most modern fields these demands tended to become based on strongly ascriptive assumptions about rights of access to the center and/or of distribution of resources from the center. The claims to these rights were couched either in terms of actual power position, such as those made by various bureaucratic or oligarchic groups, or in terms of membership in ethnic, religious or national communities; they were but rarely related—as was the case for instance in Japan—to the contribution of such groups to the center and its goals.

Thus, economic demands and policies tended very often to be perceived in terms of access to resources, positions and jobs, and much less as mechanisms developing or structuring new types of economic actions, status and class relations.

In the educational field[19] there tended to develop a continuous emphasis on getting, or providing, wider access to educational facilities, as means of unconditional access to occupational positions, and minimizing the more conditional advancement. This was very closely related to the swelling of administrative personnel and to the expansion of bureaucracies as means of coopting wider groups into the modern patrimonial center—a phenomenon which has indeed become one of the most prevalent characteristics of these societies.

In the field of agrarian reforms there also tended to develop a great upsurge of demands—very often irrespective of the actual class composition of the 'reformers'—for distribution and possibly expropriation of land with much weaker emphasis on economic development, diversification and changes in their central structural frameworks.[20]

Thus, in more general terms, there took place in most of these societies, a continuous crystallization of several political syndromes: the monopolization of central power and political resources by the center; the minimization of independent access by broader groups to such resources and to the positions controlling them; but at the same time only a minimal degree of creation by the centers or by the society of new, more differentiated, types of social organizations and institutions.

These basic political characteristics of these various regimes and their more detailed derivatives or manifestations analyzed above greatly influenced the ways in which these regimes coped with the major problems which developed within them as modern, post-traditional, orders.

The most crucial general problem which these regimes, as contrasted with the more traditional systems in general and the traditional patrimonial ones in particular (which we shall shortly analyze), have continuously been facing was the ability of their central frameworks to 'expand.' As in most other modern, post-traditional societies, the demands or expectations of such 'expansion' could develop in several different, but closely connected and interrelated, directions. First, there were the aspirations—mostly of the elites—for the creation or maintenance of new, wider, political frameworks. Second, there were the aspirations or demands for economic and/or administrative development or 'modernization.' Third, there developed the expectation for the responses, by the center, to continuously new types of demands of various new social groups. Fourth, there were the demands of these groups in general and of various new elites in particular, for incorporation into the center, for more direct access to it, for possible redefinitions of the boundaries and symbols of the collectivity, as well as for more active participation in the political process.

These demands and expectations tended to crystallize in patterns which were in a sense specific to the modern situations. First, there was the sheer increase in the quantity of such demands, which was closely related to the increase in the possible channels of access to resources—be they educational channels, or channels of access to bureaucratic or political positions. The sheer increase in the quantity of demands was also closely related to the wider range of the groups and strata which tended to become politically articulated and to make claims for various demands on the center.

However, it was not only a quantitative difference. Beyond this there developed, among broader groups, tendencies to make demands on the center in terms of the dynamics of the respective spheres in which the problems to which they addressed themselves emerged—be it agrarian problems, problems of urbanization, rise of new occupational categories, and so on. Such demands tended here, as in other modern societies, to become connected with demands in the symbolic sphere derived from the participatory and consensual orientations inherent in the very premises of modernity; hence to become articulated into themes of protest and into the broader political processes and to impinge on the very centers of the social and political orders.

It was around such various demands and around the center's responses to them that, as we shall see in greater detail later, some of the major possibilities of conflict, cleavages, and crises which could undermine the respective regimes tended to develop.

Hence also, as in all modern regimes, the possible crises of these regimes tended here as well to crystallize around combined problems of efficiency and legitimacy of the regime, i.e., around the centers' ability to deal with current policy and administrative problems, to respond to the various concrete and general demands of the more articulated groups; to incorporate new elites into the more central frameworks and broader groups into the emerging modern political framework.

CONDITIONS AND FOCI OF CLEAVAGES AND CRISES IN NEOPATRIMONIAL REGIMES

Although many of these problems of 'expansion' as they have developed in these societies are similar to those to be found in other types of modern polities, these regimes differ from the others—especially from those shaped according to the 'nation-state,' or social revolutionary (Russian, Chinese), national-revolutionary (Turkish or Mexican) or Japanese model—in the relative importance of different demands and crises. These regimes also differed from the others in the nature of the broader institutional and social conditions and cleavages which may create potential conflicts in these societies; in the more specific constellation of forces and structural mechanisms through which such broad conditions are activated so as to undermine the stability of any given neopatrimonial regime; and in several aspects of the outcomes of these crises.

One such set of conditions which influenced the stability of such regimes was related to problems having to do with the transition from a pre-colonial and/or 'traditional' society to an independent and post-traditional political order.

Among such conditions which may generate in these regimes different degrees of instability, of special importance is the possibility of discrepancies between the premises of the new broader frameworks and the political orientations of the groups active in the center, as well as of the broader groups of the population. These are due mainly first to the difficulties in the institutionalization of a relatively cohesive and flexible modern institutional center which is capable both of promoting and regulating change and which is responsive to various needs and demands without succumbing to them, and thus becoming totally ineffective. Especially important are the difficulties in the establishment and institutionalization—whether formal or informal—of fixed, acceptable rules of the political game, such as systems of election or less formal institutional devices of different types which establish some procedural consensus in the society. Also especially important are the difficulties in the establishment of relatively flexible and differentiated legal and administrative systems which whatever their social or political underpinnings, could assure some basic legal rights to individuals and some minimal political rights to citizens.

Second, these discrepancies may also be due to the relative lack of homogeneity of populations, to the weakness of tradition of political unity, and to a very weak attachment to and identification with any broader political frameworks.

Indicative of these potential discrepancies has been the fact that the rulers of these countries were often faced with the simultaneous development of different and often contradictory problems. First, they were faced with the problems of the creation of new broader political frameworks and of the acquisition of power and of maintaining themselves in power; second, with assuring the development of some general attachment to these frameworks together with the maintenance of political regulation of different issues and problems and with finding adequate ways and means of solving social, economic and political problems.

Thus, some of the potential crises specific to these regimes were often generated by the very attempts of the elites to establish and maintain a general framework of power based on some type of broader common symbols and attachment to them, or on a unified, relatively rational administration derived from former colonial frameworks.

Second, such crises could also develop through the initial attempts of many of these elites to shape the contours of these modern frameworks according to some of the imported 'nation-states' or 'revolutionary' models of modern regimes which tended to compete with each other, and which were 'alien' both to the conception of the periphery as well as to the actual behavior of these elites.

Similarly, there tended to develop here the cleavages or discrepancies between those elites and/or wider groups which attempted to uphold some types or aspects of traditional legitimations as against those which propagated a more 'modern,' nontraditional legitimation of the social and political orders.

Many of these states also faced great difficulties because of the social, ethnic, regional or religious heterogeneity of their populations which were put—unlike in the traditional patrimonial regimes—into a relatively unitary framework. Such difficulties were aggravated insofar as—despite the continuous undermining of local, 'traditional' identities—the incorporation of such regional, ethnic or religious units into some wider setting was not very effective: when these units showed little attachment or loyalty to the new settings and their symbols and were not willing to respond to demands for such loyalty couched in some such modern terms; and when consequently they could very easily develop into focal points of potentially divisive identities and collectivities.

These problems were, of course, greatly aggravated insofar as they converged with the weakness and lack of continutiy of the broader central institutional frameworks established by their new modern rulers. They become especially acute insofar as the contestants for power within these new frameworks were mostly made up of relatively small non-cohesive groups, such as groups of leaders of weak nationalistic movements, or of army and professional and bureaucratic groups and later on, technocratic ones, with but very weak commitments to any broader order or frameworks.[21]

Second these problems could be aggravated insofar as the opening up of the traditional groups was connected with only a small degree of their internal self-transformation, with a high degree of internal closeness, and with the concomitant growth of unregulated political demands and aspirations. Insofar as rapid 'detribalization' and urbanization was connected to a process of continuous erosion of the traditional frameworks, and insofar as these broader groups became disorganized and socially mobilized and drawn into the orbit of the new central modern institutions, they tended to evince the characteristics of 'closeness' and excessive political militancy.

Beyond these conditions related to problems of transition from 'underdeveloped' or 'traditional' to modern societies there were those which developed and which were connected with the more 'modern' problems such as those of economic and social development and mobilization, and of incorporation, on modern terms, of various strata and religious ethnic groups into the new polity and centers. This was first of all true with regard to problems of incorporation of various ethnic or regional groups which could become points of conflagration that could easily threaten the unitary framework of the new states and the terms of its unification.

One focus of such conflict was often, as in Indonesia and Malaya,[22] the possibility of monopolization—much beyond the traditional 'segregative' practice—of the new centers by only one or two regions, with the consequent intensification of interregional conflicts and secessional attitudes.

Similarly, given the impetus created by the new modern institutional premises, segregated ethnic groups—occupying special structural, economic or religious enclaves which gave them some special (or independent) economic power—tended to demand full participation in the new polity and a full access to the center, according to the models of universalistic citizenship upheld by these regimes. In this way there could develop a situation—as in Indonesia, Ceylon or Malaya—in which the new central elites felt threatened in their control over centers of resources and power.

Such conflicts could, as in the case of the Chinese in Southeast Asia, be intensified through the existence among such groups of different (nation-state and revolutionary) political orientations and separatist parties and organizations, and through attempts to bring their international connections into their metropolis. A similar picture emerges in many of these countries with regard to the relations between religious groups and communities and their place in the political process.[23]

Here as in other modern regimes cleavages and crises could also develop through the evolving—under the conditions of growing social mobilization seemingly similar to those in other modern societies—of new economic and occupational strata, whether through various new urban groups, technocratic elements in the center or through changes in the agrarian sector.

22

But the relatively greater importance of such ethnic, religious and regional cleavages is not the most important of such regimes' specific characteristics.

These specific characteristics could first of all be seen in the fact that, as we have already briefly alluded to above, all these groups evinced in these societies rather special orientations and organizational patterns which were distinct from those prevalent in other modern regimes.

Thus, for instance, the religious problems were not, in these societies —as in 'nation-states'—perceived in terms of the general commitment to a religious or a secular order or in terms of the ways in which, within such an order independent, autonomous religious groups with their own autonomous bases could maintain their independence. Rather the various religious groups tended to make claims for unconditional access to the center or to the distribution of centrally controlled resources and positions —claims which could easily merge into demands of redefining the boundaries and symbols of the collectivity. Truly enough, at first sight, their demands and organizations may seem superficially akin to the 'consociational' European system—such as in Holland or Belgium.[24] However, unlike in these systems, the potential cleavages around religious, regional and socioeconomic issues were not here especially oriented towards the access to universalistic frameworks, but rather to the establishment of closed segregated particularistic units or sectors.

A similar picture emerges with regard to the cleavages and crises around economic and social problems which tended to develop in these societies.

The major groups which developed claims around economic problems were indeed mostly of a modern kind, such as urban proletarian professionals or students. Even the agrarian problems—of which there were also many in the traditional-patrimonial regimes—tended to take on a more modern guise, a more generalized ideological orientation.

But unlike in other modern societies, the major demands of these groups were not oriented to the 'reconstruction' of the social and political order as implied in the nation-state and 'class-society' model. Rather, these demands for change were couched in terms of the incorporation of various segments of urban-rural, regional or professional sectors, professional or army cliques, and the new central distributive frameworks; around possible changes and extension in lines of dependency and patronage; around the relative terms of unconditionality of their access to various positions, e.g., the amount of 'reserved' places in bureaucracy or in educational appropriation or re-allocation of property-units.

But perhaps an even more important specific characteristic of these so-called neopatrimonial regimes which distinguished them from other types of modern or post-traditional regimes—and the nature of the structural channels through which these potentialities for conflict become articulated into more specific 'boiling points'—are the conditions under which such conflicts or cleavages are activated to a degree which may undermine the stability of these regimes.[25]

The organizational channels through which those conflicts developed so as to give possible rise to the various crises were: first, coalitions of cliques and elite groups—be they party, bureaucratic, army or 'religious' cliques; second, the extension of new lines of patronage and clientele and of possible incorporation of new types of groups into the central coalitions; third, the combination of these first two with demands made by broader social groups or categories—occupational, educational, regional, religious or ethnic—as well as with demands of these groups for access into the polity and for possible redistribution of power.

These structural channels tended to break down and the potential conflicts and cleavages activated and crystallized into full scale crises under special conditions which to some degree at least are specific to these regimes.

One such point of crystallization of crises, specific to these regimes, is the development of even short-run discrepancy between the levels of resources available for relatively immediate distribution to various groups in the population and the current bases of expectation and legitimation of the system.

Although the levels of such demands could be relatively low as compared with more 'developed' societies, yet both because all these demands tended to be oriented to the center as well as because of the strong distributional and paternalistic assumptions of these demands, the threshold of tolerance of deprivation or 'deferral of gratification' tended here to be low. Hence, a decline in such levels of resources—either because of 'objective' (such as bad crops, international economic fluctuation) reasons, or because of a rise in the current level of expectations as a result of the contradictory promises of elites—may, if combined with the preceding types of cleavages, give rise to the 'breaking down' of the structural channels of political struggle analyzed above.

Another condition under which such structural points could be activated is when the elites in general and contending elites in particular tend to mobilize an overflow of demands for different types of resources towards the center and are not able to segregate the demands for access to different types of central resources (such as economic resources, political participation and prestige) within each segment of the population and minimize their simultaneous overflow into the center.

Given the combination of the structural breaking points of the major channels and participants in the political struggle and the boiling points of possible crises, it can be better understood why there tended to develop, in situations of crises in these societies, the basic characteristics of 'breakdowns.'

It was not only that these situations were very often characterized by high incidence of violence, by relatively violent uprisings and coups. Beyond this they could also often be characterized by a disjunction between the levels of aspiration of different groups and the possibilities of their implementation; by a tendency to a high level of dissociation between different elites—be they regional or common central, solidary and instrumental ones; and by the technical inadequacy of the regulative mechanisms to deal with the rising levels of conflicts, and by the inadequacy of the broader symbols to uphold attempts at the institutionalization of such regulative mechanisms.[26]

Thus in general the stability of these regimes is dependent first on the degree to which the various types of conflicts and cleavages which are specific to them is small; second—whatever the level of such conflicts—on the degree that the relations among elites and between them and broader strata is structured in such a way as not to raise the level of demands on resources and so as not to break the continuation of segregative cooperation between elites.

As in other political regimes in general and modern ones in particular —the weakening of cooperation between elites gives rise to conflicts and to crises. However, unlike in other types of modern societies, the type of cohesion and interaction which brings such elites or groups into continuous intensive, cross-cutting contacts may be very detrimental to the stability of these regimes. So long as the segregation between different types of demands can be maintained and/or insofar as the pressure on the resources is minimized, the possibility of a development of a full blown crisis is usually small.

VARIETIES OF NEOPATRIMONIAL REGIMES AND THE NATURE OF POLICIES AIMING TO ASSURE THEIR STABILITY

The various characteristics of the political structure and process analyzed above can be found in most of the neopatrimonial regimes. But beyond them are developed many different types of such regimes which evinced also great differences in the concrete patterns of this process.

While many differences among these regimes may, of course, be listed, four major types seem to be of special importance. One is the 'degree' of technical and economic developments in levels of 'social mobilization' and the composition of social groups and strata within them.

Second, are differences in the differential emphasis on some of the various broader orientations to the political and cultural order, which tend to be prevalent in these societies. Third, are differences in the degree of upholding traditional, as against some more 'modern' legitimation. Fourth, are differences in the cohesiveness of the major elites of these societies, in the degree of attachment of its population to the frameworks of the polity, in the self-conception of the elites and broader-strata in these societies, especially, but not only, in terms of modernizing and development goals and social orientations and ideologies.

The differences in the levels of technical and economic developments, and of 'social mobilization' and structural differentiation that were prevalent within these regimes range from relatively 'low' levels in Syria and some Latin American countries (like Paraguay), through somewhat higher levels in the Maghreb and Southeast Asian countries (where there also existed rather far-reaching differences), up to relatively higher levels in Malaysia, Ceylon, and the more developed Latin American countries like Argentina, Chile or Brazil.[27]

These differences were related to, although not necessarily identical with, those in the composition of the major social groups. Obviously, the higher the level of economic development the greater also, on the whole, the degree to which modern occupational categories tended to develop.

But often with relatively similar levels of 'development' there could yet develop rather important differences in the occupational or social composition of such categories.

One such important difference was in the degree of 'uprootedness' or decomposition of rural and urban groups alike. The former could be connected, as in India, Ceylon or Malaysia, with rural overpopulation. The latter tended to develop—albeit in different degrees—in countries such as Indonesia, Ceylon, and Morocco, where there was widespread migration to cities within which there were very few occupational—especially industrial—openings.[28]

Another important difference was in the composition of the higher and middle 'classes.' Here of special importance was, first, the extent to which there existed within these countries former (often traditionalist) 'oligarchic' landowner and commercial elements, or even, as in Southeast Asian countries, aristocratic elements; second, in the degree to which there existed within the middle class proper some 'independent' commercial, industrial or professional groups, as in Ceylon and Malaysia, as against the preponderance of bureaucratic-administrative elements; and third, in the degree to which such economically independent elements might have been composed, as in Malaysia, Indonesia, and to some degree the Maghreb and Latin American countries, of foreign ethnic elements.

Fourth, is the relative importance of different types of intellectual groups that tend to develop in these societies, whether 'traditional,' religious, or more modern intellectual, professional and technocratic ones; the relative strength and political orientations of both these groups—and within the latter the relative importance of technocratic and professional elements; and last, the extent to which such elements are independent from both the traditional (religious) or the political (state) powers.

A similar wide range of differences can be found among these different neopatrimonial regimes with respect to the relative importance of predominance of the different orientations which, as we have seen above, tended to develop in these societies. Thus they could differ greatly as to the degree to which the 'resource' attitude to the social order and center was combined with a more passive acceptance of the premises of cultural and social orders alike, as against the perception of the possibility of more active participation or change within them.

Thus, in Southeast Asia and in the more traditional Islamic countries, there seems to have persisted a relatively passive attitude at least towards the givenness of the cultural order, but with different degress of politization and political activity; in many of the Middle Eastern countries the givenness of the cultural order constituted a major focus of controversy. In the Latin American countries we find already a much more active attitude with regard both to participation in the cultural and the political order—even if the cultural order could still be conceived either as 'given' or, as in Middle Eastern countries, a focus of controversy.

In other countries, such as in the Philippines, there seems to have developed a much lesser emphasis on the 'givenness' of the cultural order and a much greater openness towards its content, connected with growing secularization and yet not necessarily connected with any greater degree of commitment to it in terms of broader, transcendental values.

These differences influenced—often in ways similar to other modern societies—many aspects of the social structure of the political process of these societies.

Thus, on the whole, the less fully organized parties and more restricted types of cliques tend to develop mostly in societies with loose levels of social mobilization, while more continuous types of political organization in general, and most fully organized parties in particular, tend to develop mostly within societies with a higher degree of social mobilization.

Similarly, the types of public outbursts tend to vary from rather sporadic and unorganized, even if often recurrent, to more continuous and widespread populist movements such as those found in the more developed or differentiated sectors, e.g., many of the Latin American countries or the urban sectors of Southeast Asia.

But the more restricted and unstable cliques could also become relatively predominant within the more 'developed' sectors, insofar as they were characterized by a small degree of cohesion within the center as well as a high degree of uprootedenss of the various groups. The latter, obviousl greatly influenced the frequency of outbursts and the general predilection violence.

The degree of social mobilization naturally also influenced the types of problems which tended to develop in these societies. Thus in societies with relatively low levels of mobilization most such problems were focused either around interclique relations together with some problems in the agrarian sectors and some urban overpopulation, while those problems which related to urban or to industrial settings tended to become more important with the growth of social mobilization. But a high degree of up-rootedness tended to increase greatly the degree to which even such problems could become more visible and the elites more sensitive to them.

The visibility of such problems, and their articulation into political demands, were usually also enhanced by a high level of politization in the society—due either to the weakening of centers and/or the breakdown of traditional legitimation. The importance of these factors could be especially seen with regard to educational problems and demands, which in many of these societies tended to erupt not necessarily in relation to degrees of structural or economic differentiation, but also as a result of growing political mobilization—often irrespective of economic differentiation.

Similarly, the ways in which these issues and problems were political articulated were dependent to a very high degree on the relative importance within each society of the different orientations or codes characteristic of patrimonial regimes.

Thus, to give just one illustration: in those societies in which there prevailed a passive attitude to the social order—as in Burma or Indonesia—there tended to develop less fully organized types of political groups and more sporadic movements, and political demands tended to be rather diffuse and not fully articulated. In those societies with a more active orientation to the social order, like the Philippines, there tended to develop more continuous types of political organization and more articulated types of political demands.

The combination of these variables also influenced the overall pattern of political struggle within these regimes. Thus, in societies with low levels of differentiation and relatively traditional centers, the political struggle could very often focus around problems of inter-clique relations, on the one hand, and the placation of some of the groups which were able to stage ad hoc outbursts, on the other. The political issues in these societies were mostly segregated, discrete, and but rarely continuous and fully articulated politically. Within societies with higher levels of mobilization the political struggle could center around a wide range of problems or demands, while the degree to which such demands could become related to broader demands for incorporation into the center depended mostly on the level of politization and the more concrete patterns of demands prevalent in these societies.

Similarly, these conditions influenced the types of coalition that tend to develop in these societies; thus, in the less 'developed' societies such coalitions tend to be rather similar to those in 'traditional' patrimonial societies—small palace groups around the king, or loose cliques of army officers, the bureaucracy, and leaders of family and regional groups. In the more 'developed' of these societies, such coalitions tend to comprise a potentially wider range of such elite groups—including professional and urban elites, as well as looser parties and populistic leaders.

At all levels of 'differentiation' such political struggles could often be connected with changes of regime in institutional or constitutional terms. The details of such changes would vary greatly between such different regimes depending on their formal constitutions, but of special importance are constitutional—presidential or parliamentary—regimes changing to more 'arbitrary' ones—whether unitary regimes, or various 'usurpatory' ones in which some branches of the government, usually the executive branch, would usurp powers which are not granted them in the constitution. Very often this would be done in the name of safeguarding the constitution.

In almost all such regimes, especially insofar as the center was composed of weak and contending groups and there was a weak institutional framework, the army could come to play a very important role in the struggle. But, as we shall see in greater detail later on, the social and political orientation of the army may vary greatly in different situations.

Many of those differences among the different regimes and their effects on the political process were not dissimilar from those that can be found in other types of modern regimes.

But whatever the differences between such different neopatrimonial regimes, they all shared the specific general characteristics outlined above, and in all of them the stability of the regimes was greatly dependent on the maintenance of the specific patterns of 'segregation' between groups, strata and elites, which were analyzed above.

But such conditions are never fully assured and one of the major policies of the various ruling elites of such regimes was to assure maintenance of such conditions. Of special importance here were their attempts to control and regulate the political process in their respective societies—

its major issues and organizations—in such a way that it would not impinge on their monopoly of central political power and would not enable the development, by different groups, of independent access to sources of society-wide power.

The rulers attempted to minimize the possibilities of the development of new political orientations, demands for new types of political participation, or new concepts of political symbolism—and as far as such new political concepts and organizations tended to develop, to suppress or segregate them.

The political struggle could be limited in these societies to such organizational levels and issues insofar as it was possible to maintain within these societies several types of 'segregation' or limitation of contacts between the basic constituent units of these societies.

Hence the central elites attempted to regulate the flow of each such type of resources thorughout the society. They attempted especially to minimize the possibility that different groups would engage, on a society or region-wide basis, in the free and simultaneous exchange of different types of resources, especially of the combination of kinship and religious ones with political or economic ones, and in this way create for themselves more independent access to central frameworks.[29]

In more concrete terms the elites of these societies attempted to limit the contacts among the different units of the periphery and between them and the center to mostly adaptive or external relations.

Second, and probably more important from the point of view of our analysis, were the attempts to minimize the free flow of such society-wide resources—and especially those of society-wide solidarity—and political interrelations.

Third, was the limitation of any broader contacts which might have developed among the different units mainly to one type of resource or sphere—be it economic, 'religious' or kinship.

Given that all these regimes evinced some characteristics which differentiated them from those of other modern regimes, to what extent is it at all meaningful to term them patrimonial? To what degree do they evince some similarities to the traditional patrimonial regimes? We shall therefore now turn to the analysis of these regimes.

III. TRADITIONAL PATRIMONIAL REGIMES

THE POLITICAL FORMAT OF TRADITIONAL PATRIMONIAL REGIMES

The traditional patrimonial regimes have also existed within a great range of societies.[30] Among these the more important have been the earlier kingdoms in the Near and Middle East, such as the Ancient Egyptian Empire, Assyrian and Babylonian Kingdoms and smaller empires, like ancient Akkad, the many nomad kingdoms or 'empires' ranging from relatively loose tribal conquerors such as those of the Hyxos and Hittites, up to the more fully organized ones of the Mongols, most of the first Germanic and Slavic tribes that settled in Europe, many of the Indian and Southeast Asian and to some extent also Middle American kingdoms, as well as probably many of the medieval Balkan and Slavic states mentioned above. Possibly also several embryonic types of such political systems could be found in Polynesia.

The first, and probably the most important area or sphere in which some such similarities can be found, is—as in the neopatrimonial regimes—in the structure of centers of these societies and in the relations between center and periphery, as well as in the whole format of political organization that was prevalent in these societies.

The major specific characteristic of the centers of patrimonial (as distinct from other 'archaic' or 'historical') regimes is that while the difference between center and periphery which tended to develop in the patrimonial regimes was very high as compared to primitive tribal societies, or to simple city states, yet it was low as compared to Imperial societies or fully developed city states. Such difference was mostly one of ecological and symbolic distinction rather than of fully symbolic or structural differentiation.

Truly enough, the centers which the rulers of traditional patrimonial regimes tried to establish in administrative cities and/or temple-cities, or sometimes—as in North Africa—in rather shifting sites or the seats of religious and political mediators (and in which the rulers attempted to establish great monuments of centrality, in the form of temples and palaces[31])—were conceived by these rulers, even if they were weak and transient, as distinct from the periphery, as different from it and barely accessible to it.

The major nucleus of these centers was usually the household of the prince or ruler, or a priestly group. Within these centers there did indeed develop a much higher degree of concentration of population, and of internal division of labour and specialization than in the periphery. Within the centers the relatively undifferentiated kinship units that were predominant in the periphery became weakened and there soon took place a concomitant growth of more specialized units—such as craft and merchant organizations, some groups of labourers and especially of new administrative and ritual organizations.

And yet, however powerful these centers were, however great the distinctiveness and distance of the center from the periphery (and in many of these societies, as for instance, in the Southeast Asian ones, it could be very great), there developed within these societies but few structural differences between the center and the periphery, and the differentiation between center and periphery was based mainly on ecological distinctiveness and on greater concentrations of populations.[32]

The degree of specialization as well as the degree of the internal autonomy of the urban communities was, especially as compared with other types of urban concentration in the traditional post-tribal societies, rather limited.

These limitations were due to the wide predominance of the kinship-based royal household or of religious lineages and cults in the governance and organization of these cities—a predominance which tended to overwhelm and limit the more specialized units and activities.

Hence in most capitals of patrimonial regimes, the commercial or manufacturing activities were either secondary or non-existent; and their absence sometimes undermined the possibility of maintaining any stable administrative political center. In some patrimonial regimes these economic activities were performed outside the capital cities in different types of international enclaves—i.e., caravan-cities, temple-centers, some city-states—or were delegated to typical secondary cities.

This nature of the limited differentiation or distinction between the center and periphery in these societies can best be seen in the nature of the kinship and family symbols that were prevalent in them.

Such symbols—be they those of family solidarity or succourance—played a prominent role in the defining of overall sociopolitical identity of most traditional patrimonial societies. The macro-societal order was in these regimes usually conceived in terms of such symbols.

But the nature of these familial and kinship symbols and structures differs here greatly from those of various other 'primitive,' 'tribal,' 'kinship' societies. These symbols and structures have become here much more abstract and generalized and they already imply some difference between concrete closed kinship units and the broader society.

But however diluted the kinship structures and symbolism were in these societies, the basic conception of the social order and the cosmic orders held up by the center—as also that of the periphery, even when not couched entirely in terms of symbols of kinship— were usually based on some conception of homology between the social and the cosmic orders or of a separation between them.

Hence the cosmic order which the center represented was not entirely different from that of the periphery—although it was conceived as more encompassing and more articulate than that of the periphery.

Truly enough, insofar as there emerged some distinction between the ritual-religious and the political centers (as in parts of Catholic Europe and in Buddhist monarchies of South East Asia), there also developed some tensions between those religious elites and the rulers who wanted to monopolize the representation of the central symbols of the society. But all such struggles were waged basically within the confines of a symbolic system or order which, however rationalized or developed as compared with more primitive ones, either still assumed a homology or parallelism between them, or, at most—as in the cases of Buddhist and Catholic centers, based on transcendental religious orientations—emphasized a distinction and segregation between the social and cosmic order.

Accordingly, the conception of the center that was prevalent in these societies stressed its role as the keeper of a static, social and cosmic order, in whose hands was vested the upholding of this order and of the wellbeing and order of the society; and the activities and policies developed by the central elites were strongly derived from this conception.

The basic premises of these activities were the attempts of the central elites to: maintain in the hands of the center the monopoly of central political activities and resources; limit any independent access of the periphery to them; and minimize the direct, independent, political contact and participation of the periphery in the center.[33]

These premises were reflected first of all in the society-wide activities of the center which were most predominant in these societies. The central elites attempted here first to assure for themselves the monopoly of symbolizing the direct relation between cosmic and social order, especially insofar as these symbols were related to political organizations. Second, these elites attempted to hold most of the 'external' relations in their own hands, or at least, to control such relations of the various sub-units of the society. Last, internally, these elites focused on providing the various groups and strata of their respective societies with various internal adaptive 'facilities,' especially those of mediation and upholding of peace on the one hand, and of accumulation, provision and distribution of economic resources, on the other.

As contrasted with these activities, other possible types of activities of the center—such as the development of symbols of a new common political and cultural identity, the crystallization of autonomous political-collective goals, or the development of new types of intergroup relations and of frameworks regulating such relations, all of which were indeed very prominent in Imperial or city-states—were only of secondary importance in patrimonial societies.

Accordingly, the central elites tended to develop here policies which were mostly prescriptive and regulative. They developed but very few promotive ones, i.e., those which were oriented not only to accumulation and distribution of power resources or to the mediation between different groups, but also to the creation or promotion of new types of activities, or of serving various groups on their own terms.[34]

Among these prescriptive and regulative policies, of special importance were those aiming at the accumulation, in the hands of the centers, of the available resources and of the monopolization by the center of their possible distribution among the various groups of the society. Also, insofar as the rulers of these regimes engaged in economic policies, these were: first, to use Hoselitz's[35] nomenclature, mostly of expansive character, i.e., aiming at expansion of control of large territories, rather than intrinsic ones (characterized by intensive exploitation of a fixed resource basis): and second, to use K. Polany's terms, these policies were mostly redistributive ones.[36]

Thus, in many of these societies—and especially in the more compact ones—the central elites attempted to control the ownership of land either by vesting all the ownership in their own hands and making most of the peasant families into tenants of sorts and/or by supervising and controlling the degree to which the various plots of land which were still owned by different kinship units could be transferred freely. Such policies were indeed in sharp contrast to those of the Emperors in many centralized Imperial systems who have often attempted to weaken the position of the aristocracy by promoting a relatively free peasantry.

Such distributive and extractive policies—often coupled with the performance of ritual acts aiming at the maintenance of the harmony between the cosmic and the social orders—were quite in line with the ideal 'image' of the King as the 'keeper' of the welfare of the people and they were also the policies which provided the most important resources for the maintenance of the ruler's power in the internal political game.

The nature of the relatively limited extent of structural and symbolic difference between the center and the broader peripheral groups or regions of society, connected as it was with the great ecological and symbolic distance of the center, was perhaps most clearly seen in the nature of the links between the center and the periphery that tended to develop in these patrimonial regimes. The most important characteristic of these links was that they created little basic structural change within either sectors or strata of the periphery or within the center itself.[37]

The center impinged on the local (rural, urban or tribal) communities, mainly in the form of administration of law, attempts to maintain peace, exaction of taxation and the maintenance of some cultural and/or religious links to the center. But, with very few exceptions, most of these links were effected through the existing local kinship—territorial and ritual—units and subcenters. These links were mostly of rather 'external' and adaptive character, and they were to create new structural channels which undermined or attempted to change the existing social and cultural patterns of either the center or of the periphery, as was the case in Imperial systems.

This can perhaps be most clearly seen in the nature and scope of the specific legal activities developed by the patrimonial rulers.[38] These were usually confined to criminal and administrative (tax) law, to special religious laws and only to a very limited degree to the development of civil and contractual law. In these latter fields, such centers tended to uphold whatever arrangements had been developed by the various local groups or subcenters, but they did not attempt to develop new autonomous common legal and political frameworks and orientations as was the case in Imperial systems.

Thus these societies were characterized by what, in Durkheim's terms, may be called a quantitative extension of the units of 'mechanical' solidarity, in which the centers mostly attempted to provide continuous maintenance of some broad political and administrative frameworks within which the various local units could retain their own boundaries and activities.

The preponderance of these activities and policies of the center greatly influenced the nature of mechanisms of political struggle that were predominant within these centers. The most important of these mechanisms were the 'computative' ones and those of direct bargaining between various groups, rather than the more representative activities which promoted continuous uniform activities according to some general, universalistic principles of allocations or those based on the pursuance of articulated, differentiated political goals.[39]

Similarly, the main participants in the political struggle in these societies were the direct representatives of the basic groups in the center and in the periphery (kinship, territorial, religious, personal or family groups); they tended to be organized in cliques, competing for access to the royal household, creating continuously shifting and cross-cutting allegiances and coalitions with each other. The major issues and mechanisms of political struggle on the part of 'higher' (central and aristocratic) as well as 'lower' (peripheral) groups were petitions and pressures on the center to coopt new elements into the central cliques and/or change their composition: to change the details of the distribution by the center of various resources to the major groups; as well as to extend the lines of clientele and patronage.

It is here also that some of the most crucial aspects of patrimonialism so often emphasized since Weber—the famous absence of a 'rational' bureaucracy in the structure of central administration—can be seen in their true perspectives.

The lack of 'rationality' of these administrations does not necessarily refer to the limitation in the scope, range or complexity of its activities and organization. These could often be very encompassing and great. Rather, 'lack of rationality' of such administrations refers to the nature of the goals of action and criteria according to which its activities—however wide and complex—were organized. These were focused around 'ad hoc,' particularistic, regulative and distributive, rather than on the more continuous, and universalistic criteria, and it is these predominances of such criteria which tended to promote the 'non-rational' or 'non-professional' aspects of these administrations.

It is also within the context of these characteristics of the center and its relations to the periphery that the specific importance of 'personalist' rule can be best understood. The possibility of government being based in these societies on often-shifting personal allegiances has indeed been inherent in the structure of these centers—especially in the relatively low level of political commitment towards them, in the strong emphasis on the external and adaptive functions of the center, and in the adaptive and external relation between the center and the periphery. But the exact extent to which such shifting personal allegiance—as opposed to a more stable, routinized, hereditary, or other-type of rule—became predominant in a given patrimonial regime depended very much on the concrete constellation of different forces within it. Thus, the tendency to personalistic rule more than the constituting 'essence' of these regimes, was rather the extreme—and to some degree most visible—manifestation of some possibilities inherent in their basic structural characteristics.

These characteristics of relations between center and periphery that were prevalent in the traditional patrimonial regimes also greatly influenced the very conception of the political boundaries of political community, in their relation to cultural and 'social' or ethnic ones, that tended to develop within these societies.

Unlike in many city-states, or especially in Imperial systems, there did not develop in these societies a strong emphasis on the necessity of convergence of these different boundaries in one territorial framework and around one territorial focus or center. Hence, there tended also to develop a relatively weak symbolic attachment to frontiers and to territory. However strong the attempts of the rulers to maintain the frontiers of their domain, frontiers were not perceived in terms of the basic cultural identity of the collectivity.[40]

Both the center and the periphery of these societies could identify themselves with many different points of reference, with many cultural or ethnic symbols, with several different Great Traditions, each with a different territorial boundary. Different regimes, family or other groups, might have different foci of territorial identity, often dividing and shifting their allegiance between different cultural or religious centers, and hence these allegiances could be relatively easily transferred from one territorial focus, or center, to another.

THE VARIETY OF TRADITIONAL PATRIMONIAL REGIMES

As in the case of the 'modern' neopatrimonial regimes, there developed also a great variety of traditional patrimonial regimes. They could differ according to several criteria. First they could differ according to the size and scope of the respective patrimonial domains and centers.

Second, these regimes could also greatly differ with regard to the relative strength of their central political and administrative frameworks. Thus, for instance, in the less organized of such regimes—closer to the tribal federations of North Africa—there developed very weak[41] administrative centers, even if they were, at the same time, carriers of special religious functions and related to transcendental, universalistic religion. In other such loose centers, such as in ancient Middle Eastern tribal federations, the patrimonial elites displayed almost exclusive concern for the preservation of the existing weak frameworks of power; they performed some administrative and mediating functions, without simultaneously maintaining any strong commitment to a religious order, performing but minimal religious functions.[42]

Third, there were differences in the levels of technological development and economic productivity, again ranging from such 'low' levels of development as a desert tribal federation or kingdom, up to the highly organized hydraulic societies, such as the first Egyptian Empire and the Ceylonese Kingdom.[43]

Fourth, they could also greatly vary according to the relative scope and strength of the solidarity of the ruling elite—and in its relations with the periphery.

Fifth, there were differences in the nature of the religious systems which were prevalent among them. These have ranged from relatively 'simple' semi-primitive religions embedded in kinship and local units and symbols as in many local Southeast Asian domains, up to such 'high' or 'great' religions as Buddhism, with a very strong personal-transcendental element or orientation within them; or up to some Roman Catholic countries such as the Spanish American Empire where the tradition of natural law helped indeed to uphold many patrimonial elements, but at the same time did also uphold, at least in the more private sphere, many of the transcendental orientations inherent in the Christian framework.

Similarly, there tended to develop great differences in the relations between the political and the religious centers in these societies according to their relative strength or weakness, and according to their relative dominance over each other. On the one hand there could develop many of the weak Middle Eastern polities, while on the other hand, there could also develop, as in several Southeast Asian societies, or in Ahmenid Persia or Indian States,[44] strong political centers which succeeded in assuring for themselves the monopoly or control of the religious symbolism.

These differences were closely related to the relative strength of the major participants in the political struggle: the kind, with wider political groups, such as the traditional aristocratic groups, or other more 'flexible' religious or urban groups. These differences had many repercussions on various aspects of these respective regimes, and especially on the extent of articulation and development of different aspects of political processes within them.

But whatever the success of any such attempts, there might have easily developed within these regimes, under the impact of the internal and external forces alike, cleavages which could have undermined the stability of such regimes and given rise to conflicts, demise and change.

The major cleavages which would develop in these societies tended to coalesce around, first, regional and religious allegiances; second, around the conflicts of different strata within the periphery—especially between urban and rural, but also between different groups within cities and country side; and third, and last, around possible conflicts and dissensions within the elite groups closest to the center or active within it.

The concrete lines of such cleavages differed greatly among such different patrimonial regimes, to some degree according to the relative constellation of forces analyzed in the preceding section. It was insofar as these lines of cleavage tended to coalesce that the stability of any given patrimonial regime could become undermined, giving rise to its demise and to the development 'on its ruins' of other regimes.

Several major directions of such change within, and of, such regimes can be pointed out.[45]

First, there was the possibility of personal, dynastic, or territorial changes without any great changes in the basic nature of the regimes. This possibility was probably most frequent when there were relatively strong political centers which were able to maintain their own continuity and which served as foci of attractiveness for various, especially aristocratic, groups.

Second, and especially in the case of weak centers, there was the possibility, as can be seen in the Eastern European and Southeast Asian cases, of dismemberment of any given patrimonial system into several other patrimonial units, into what may be called a special type of 'segmented territorial succession.'

In both cases such changes were often connected with purely personal or family changes within the ruling groups or with a high degree of turnover of ruling personnel within them. The degree and concrete direction of any such change was greatly dependent on some of the variables, as we have seen above, on which the various traditional patrimonial regimes tended to differ among themselves.

Very often such changes gave rise to the development, from within a relatively weak patrimonial regime, of a stronger, more unified one, or to important shifts in the structure of the ruling group, or to the relative predominance of secular as against religious groups.

However great these changes might have been, insofar as the new regime could also maintain the segregated balance between the different structural and territorial forces of which they were composed, and insofar as they did not undermine the predominance of the constellation of patrimonial codes, these changes did not 'touch' on some of the basic-symbolic and organization cores of these systems and on their basic structural derivatives—such as the definition of the boundaries of collective identities and the relation between such collective identities and the foci of personal identity, the basic relation between center and periphery, and the overall format of political struggle.

It was only insofar as there developed, among the groups and strata which gave rise to such cleavages, also strong groups which were organized according to some orientations and structural principles markedly differing from those prevalent in the patrimonial regimes, that the changes which arose out of these cleavages gave rise to new nonpatrimonial types of new systems.

This possibility was most frequent in cases when such changes were connected with great heterogeneity in the composition of the constituent units of such regimes and especially insofar as among such heterogeneous elements there were also relatively strong, independent, political or religious groups and elites which could serve as foci for new charismatic orientations and centers, on the one hand, and/or commercial or manufacturing groups which could serve as bases for more differentiated resources, on the other hand.

In such cases there developed the possibility of combining personal dynastic and territorial changes with the developments of new structural or cultural orientations (codes). It was insofar as such forces did develop that the transformation of patrimonial systems into more differentiated types of polities, first of all into Imperial or feudal systems, but also into other sub-units or enclaves, like city-state, could take place.

IV. CONDITIONS OF DEVELOPMENT AND CONTINUITY OF TRADITIONAL AND MODERN PATRIMONIAL REGIMES

The preceding analysis indicates that many similarities can be found in some of the basic characteristics of traditional and post-traditional patrimonial regimes, and especially in the modes of coping with the central problems of political life. How can we then explain these similarities? And how are they related to the 'seemingly' obvious differences between traditional and modern regimes?

One central clue to this similarity, as well as to the differences between them, can be found in the conditions of the development and continuity of these types of regimes. As has been emphasized above, the traditional patrimonial regimes were only one type of society or political system that developed among so-called archaic or historical societies. Hence, there naturally arises the question or problem about the specific conditions under which they developed.

As in the development of other types of archaic or historical societies, the most important conditions here were a combination of internal and international circumstances. Although it is not easy to specify the exact combination of these forces which gave rise to that system—as distinct from other types of 'traditional' political systems—some indication may not be out of place. Among the most important conditions of the development of these types of regimes have probably been the growth of contacts between various units characterizing relatively low levels of differentiation, and the possibility of their becoming dependent on some cooperation for defense or for the maintenance of some common technological frameworks (like common works of irrigation).

The push to such contacts tended here usually to come either from some external events or forces—such as movements of population or change in technology which facilitated the development of techniques of agricultural cultivation and made more extensive trade relations possible—or from an internal force: the push of political elites to territorial expansion. It was these changes which enabled, with the growing accumulation of various resources, the developments in the political and symbolic fields which were analyzed above.

The development, out of such contacts of patrimonial as against other types of 'archaic' or 'historical' societies, was facilitated or predicated by the prevalence within the societies of certain types of kinship as well as of broader socio-cultural orientations.

Such kinship units were characterized by some type of bilateral or multilateral kinship arrangements; by a relatively low scope of solidarity and continuity of broader kinship (lineage or even broader family) units; by nonperpetuation of such units through primogeniture or similar arrangements; by the tendency to equal division of its holdings; by multilateral kinship networks; and by frequent use of maternal symbolism in the central symbols of these societies. (Maternal symbols seem to emphasize the 'defense' orientation against outside elements while at the same time to minimize the obligatory commitments towards these outside units.)[46]

These aspects of kinship structures have very often been connected in these societies with a specific set of conceptions of broader kinship solidarity and of the obligation it may entail. Such solidarity tended to be based on a relatively low and narrow level of mutual trust and a range of unconditional obligations and commitments. The relation to such broader units has been mostly conceived in terms of the adaptive aspects of kinship and family relations, and much less in terms of mutual commitment to such a kinship order or to a broader order of which such kinship relations were a crucial part or element. The range of such solidarity tended to be continuously shifting in its scope, as, according to the famous Arab saying: "We against my brother; me and my brother against my cousin; my brother and cousin against the stranger," etc.

The development, out of such contacts, of the patrimonial regime was greatly facilitated insofar as certain types of cultural orientations were predominant among their elites and broader strata.

First among these orientations was a relatively low level of commitment to a broader social or cultural order, a perception of this order mostly as something to be mastered or adapted to, but not as commanding a high level of commitment on behalf of those who participate in it, or who are encompassed by it.

A second orientation was a strong emphasis on the *givenness* of the cultural and social order, of a lack of perception of active autonomous participation of any of the social groups in the shaping of the contours of the order—even to the extent that such shaping is possible in traditional systems. The major groups and elites of these societies rarely conceived themselves as actively responsible for the shaping of those contours—however important they may have been in the upholding of such given orders and arrangements—as evident, for instance, in the strong emphasis on magical and ritual functions in relation to these orders.

A third orientation was either the lack of the conception of tension between a 'higher' transcendental order and the social order or—when such tension was indeed conceived as a very important element in the 'religious' sphere proper—the absence or weakness of the necessity to overcome some tensions through some 'this worldly' activity (political, economic or 'scientific') oriented to the shaping of the social and political order or its transformation.

The fourth orientation, closely related to the former, was the relatively weak emphasis of the autonomous access of the major groups or strata to the major attributes of these orders. Such access was usually seen as being mediated by ascriptive individual groups or ritual experts who represented the 'given' order, and who were mostly appointed by the center or subcenters.

It was usually kinship and territorial units with such characteristics that were most easily amenable to respond to conditions of internal and international expansion, and to give rise to elites with the types of orientations analyzed above. Insofar as they were predominant in any given territory, as against more 'differentiated,' 'solidary' types of elites, as can be found in city states or tribal federations—the prospects for the establishment of patrimonial systems have been greatest.

The possibilities of the development of such political systems were also facilitated by the encounter of such units and their elites with those more differentiated 'high' or 'great' religions in which the conception of the relations between the cosmic and the sociopolitical order (although not necessarily—as for instance in Buddhism or Catholicism—with regard to other domains of the private religious realm) was characterized by the lack of any strong transcendental orientations, on tensions between them, and by the embedment of these orders in one another.

It was usually only under the conditions specified above that the different orientations tended indeed to coalesce and consequently to generate within the center and the periphery of these societies alike, but especially in the relations between them, an emphasis on certain types of orientation to power and prestige. They tended to generate a very strong emphasis on prestige based on participation in the relatively fixed, closed, ascriptive communities; on the maintenance of the standing and relative power of these communities, and on their manipulation and regulation through relation of power to each other and to the center. But this power was here mostly oriented to the maintenance of the given structure or at most to quantitative expansion of the scope and resources of the existing units, not to the creation of new types of cultural or social activities or organization.

These more general orientations or codes, as well as the more specific emphasis on these special types of power and prestige connected with those codes or derived from them, tended to give rise to the specific structural and organizational characteristics of these regimes—especially, as we have mentioned above, to the structure of centers and their relations to the periphery, to the conception of political community, and to the patterns of political struggle which were analyzed above.

It was also the development and continuity of this specific emphasis on 'restricted' power and prestige which facilitated the regulation, limitation and flow of resources between the different sectors of the society, which, as we shall see, was so important for the continuity of these regimes.

Indeed these different orientations or 'codes' did not necessarily go together. Thus, for instance, in Japan, we find a strong emphasis on the givenness of the cultural and local order, together with a very strong commitment to this order—a combination which was connected with a much more open and dynamic role of the center and the shaping of the social order. Similarly, in many traditional Imperial societies like China, which were characterized by a much larger degree of commitment by the periphery to the center, there still existed—as Weber has shown—strong secondary patrimonial tendencies which were to some degree related to more formal attitudes, to the social order, and to 'closed' solidarities, and which could yet become predominant in times of decline of these systems.[47] But it was only under the conditions specified above that these various codes tended to coalesce together in a way in which they could greatly facilitate the development of patrimonial regimes.

The development and coalescence of these codes facilitated the development of such regimes by virtue of the fact that those groups in which such codes were predominant tended to develop those specific types of structural and organizational activities which coalesced into these types of regimes.

But, as we have seen already above, the existence of such groups in itself did not assume the continuity of any such specific patrimonial regime or even of this type of regime.

Whatever the differences between these different traditional patrimonial regimes, in none of them was their continuity assured—especially given the continuous development of new and multiple groups and social forces in these societies, as well as the 'contradictions' which develop within any regime as a result of its initial instutionalization. Such continuity could be assured only insofar as there developed and were maintained special conditions, especially the various types of segregation between different groups and resources, which were analyzed above.

Hence in the traditional, as in most modern, neopatrimonial regimes, special policies had to be developed in order to assure the continuity of such systems. It is indeed in the nature of these policies, which indicate the modes of coping with political problems, that the similarities between traditional and modern patrimonial systems stand out.

The rulers attempted—in sharp contrast to city-states and tribal federations—to minimize the possibilities of the development of new political orientations and the demands for new types of political participation, or new concepts of political symbolism, and as far as such new political concepts and organizations tended to develop, to suppress or segregate them.

Hence the central elites of these, as of the neopatrimonial regimes, attempted to regulate the flow of each such type of resource throughout the society. Hence also they attempted to minimize the possibility that different groups would engage simultaneously, on a society or regionwide basis, in the free and simultaneous exchange of different types of resource —especially of the combination of kinship and religious ones with political or economic ones—and in this way create for themselves more independent access to central frameworks.[48]

Some such policies were more pronounced in the traditional patrimonial regimes. Among these are the centers' policies in the sphere of social stratification.

The centers' attempts to insure the continuity of their regimes developed also in the sphere of social stratification. Here the centers attempted to uphold certain criteria of evaluation of social roles and positions on which the conception of social hierarchy was based, and especiall first, those of relatively narrow attributes and limited styles of life represented by relatively closed groups; second, more general attributes related to a broader conception of the cosmic and social order controlled by the center; and third, functional contributions to the social order as evaluated by the central and political elites.[49]

The centers attempted also to control the macro-societal references of evaluation and access together with allowing, even encouraging, in the various groups and strata the possibility of maintaining—so long as they di not impinge on the macro-societal level—autonomous but segregated statu arrangements.

These centers tended to encourage the segregation of the styles of life and patterns of participation of different local, occupational and territorial kinship groups, and in this way to maintain the distance of the cent and its distinctiveness from various sub-centers and from the periphery.

They attempted also to reinforce, by the lack of independent access of various groups to the center, the attributes of cosmic or ritual orders represented by it and the political and religious resources controlled by it, and to minimize their attempts to convert their resources—and especial the prestige of their collectivity—into media that might have enabled then to participate in the broader societal settings.

Hence, on the one hand, in the center as well as in many subcenters of these societies there tended to develop many highly elaborated hierarchies of ranks and positions, often related to the differential access of various groups to the center.

On the other hand, however elaborate the system of rank-hierarchy in the center or subcenter, usually no strata with country-wide state consciousness tended to develop in these societies.

Closely related to these patterns of stratification and political organization were the attempts of the rulers of these societies to develop specific patterns of absorption of social units which were structurally different from those prevalent in the center or in the periphery.

We have noted above the great importance of structural enclaves, be they economic or religious, in the center and periphery of these societies. The rulers of these regimes were indeed very interested in coopting such enclaves—be they highly active, more differentiated, economic groups which could contribute to the accumulation and extraction of resources, or differentiated types of religious orders with more transcendental orientations, which could add to the lustre of these centers.

But the rulers were ready to coopt them only so long as the units were to some degree 'external' to the central structural core of these societies, so long as they did not impinge on their internal structural arrangements and especially on the basic conception of the relations between the center and the periphery. This tendency also explains the strong predisposition in many such regimes to enable ethically alien groups, which could be segregated to an even greater degree than indigenous elements, to engage in such structurally more differentiated activities.[50]

Insofar as all these attempts of the rulers were successful they gave rise to a relatively high degree of segmentation of relation between different sectors of society and a low degree of development of new types of political orientation.

The success of these tendencies could be best seen in the types of rebellions that tended to develop in many of these societies and their impact on their respective political structures. However numerous such rebellions—especially peasant or urban uprising—might have been, they have but rarely contained any strong utopian and transcendental elements oriented to the political scene. Whatever utopian orientation they might have developed was very often 'other-worldly,' stressing the unfolding of the solidarity of existing primordial communities with but very few types of new or articulated political orientations. At times (but rarely) religious and political leaders with some new political conceptions and more differentiated political skills joined them.[51]

But it is here, in the analysis of the conditions giving rise to patrimonial regimes and those which facilitate their continuity, that not only the similarities, but also the differences between the traditional and the modern patrimonial regimes stand out.

The similarities stand out first of all in the nature of the social and cultural conditions of the development of neopatrimonial regimes.

A closer examination of the conditions which facilitated the development of such post-patrimonial regimes indicates that they are, in general terms, similar to those that we have found to be crucial for the development of traditional patrimonial regimes—namely the combination of certain cultural orientations or codes with some specific structural conditions.

First of all we see that there tended to develop, or to become predominant among the elites, as well as among the broader strata of these societies, those attitudes towards the broader social order, those conceptions of sociopolitical order, or 'codes,' as well as those patterns of solidarity which, as we have seen above, facilitated the development of (traditional) patrimonial regimes.

Perhaps the most important development here was the growing perception of the social and cultural order as 'given,' whether in rather traditional terms, as in Burma or Malaysia, or in a combination of traditional symbols with populistic terms, as in most of the Middle Eastern Countries, Indonesia or Ceylon, or, according to some basic precepts of natural law, as in Catholic Latin American countries. Such givenness could be connected, as in many Southeast Asian societies, with a very low level of commitment to such a social order, or, as in some of those societies like the Latin American or Islamic, with a higher degree of commitment to it.

Second, there tended to develop in many of these countries only a minimal distinction between cultural and political order and between the civic and cultural orders, even though each of them may have had different collective boundaries.

Third, in these conceptions the tension between the social and cosmic order was conceived as very small; instead there tended to prevail, as in Southeast Asia or to a degree in the Middle East, a conception of a fusion between the two, or, as in Latin America, a separation of the different levels of activity relevant to each of them.[52]

Even in those societies, such as some Islamic or Latin American ones, in which there existed or developed a strong conception of the individuals' or communities' duties towards the moral and social order, these duties tended to be seen more and more as imposed or represented by the center and only to a very small degree could be conceived and formulated by the individuals or by various groups according to their own autonomous perception of transcendental duty and commitments.

Fourth, there tended to develop here a rather weak connection between broader universalistic (be they religious or ideological) precepts and orientations and the actual social order, and a relatively limited comitment to such orientations as against a more ritualistic participation in the cultural orders.

Fifth, there tended to develop a relatively passive attitude towards the acceptance of the basic premises of the cultural order, a strong emphasis on its givenness, as well as a relatively low level of active commitment to the political orders. However, as we have seen above, there developed many variations among these different regimes.[53]

Parallel developments can be found in the crystallization of the conception of social hierarchy and of the patterns of stratification and strata formation in these societies, which again tended to differ greatly from the 'original model' of class society imported from the West. While here again, several differences may be found among different modern patrimonial societies, some common features stand out.[54]

Structurally, the patterns of stratification of these societies were characterized by the relative weakness of independent (especially middle) sectors and by the preponderance, within such middle sectors, of service and bureaucratic elements, and, within the higher strata, of oligarchic groups.

Here, as in traditional patrimonial systems, there tended to develop a combination between attempts of the center to control all the attributes and symbols of status which are relevant to the macro-societal terms, and the segregation of the various groups or strata in relatively closed, autonomous status units.

Similarly, the bases of evaluation tended more and more to become, frist, those of upholding attributes of relatively closed groups, with a growing importance of the differences between 'modern' and 'traditional' as one of the basic distinctions of such attributes. A second basis of such an evaluation tended to become the control over resources and last, and only to a relatively smaller degree, also some functional 'performance' or 'service' as designated by the center.

Given the emphasis on such attributes as well as on the center's predilection for strong control over the access to such attributes and especially over those which could facilitate the access to the center, there tended to develop here very weak country-wide strata or class consciousness. Instead, smaller groups (territorial, semi-occupational or local) tended to become major status units, all of them developing rather strong tendencies to status segregation with but little autonomous political orientation.

Such status segregation could be of several different kinds. It could be, as in the various more traditional sectors of Southeast Asia or the Middle-East, based on the self-conception of such groups as bearers of special differential social standing, as upholding traditions or distinctive life styles that could be ascriptively defined and whose status perception is often limited to local settings. Such status segregation could also have been conceived, as especially among Latin American oligarchies but also in many of the new urban centers in Asia or Africa, in terms of their greater control of resources or conspicuous consumption. Unlike in the former case, these were only rarely couched in terms of representing special types of attributes or participation (even if ascriptively based) in a wider societal and/or cultural order. Such groups tended to place less emphasis on life styles and family continuity than the first type, and were much more open to the undertaking of new types of activities.[55]

In common with traditional patrimonial societies, there also tended to develop in these societies a strong emphasis on the combination of 'closed' restricted prestige and 'power' as the major social orientations of the elites and the groups alike. Yet, unlike in traditional patrimonial societies, however 'segregated' the various status units might have been from each other, there tended to develop among them (especially within the less traditional ones) strong and usually ascriptive orientations and references to the center. Moreover, unlike in traditional societies, these groups attempted to convert their resources into media that might enable them to participate in the broader frameworks (but mostly in the ascriptive frameworks) of the new center.

These cultural and status orientations could facilitate here, as in traditional patrimonial settings, the crystallization of neopatrimonial regimes insofar as they were carried by persistent or emergent elites charac-terized by: 'closeness' in their social and status perception; by a ritual emphasis on certain specific and very limited types of status orientations; by a conception of their own legitimation in terms of maintaining these restricted ranges of status symbols; by relatively weak centers; and by the persistence, in internal structure of the broader strata of the society, of those aspects of kinship, orientation and structure which were found above to be prevalent in the traditional patrimonial societies.

Some of these structural conditions seemingly 'simply' persisted within the traditional sectors of these societies. But of even greater inter-est, from the point of view of our analysis is their 'transfer' or independent crystallization in the more modern (colonial and post-independence) set-tings, which seemingly were characterized by other orientations.[56]

Among the agencies or mechanisms which developed in this setting and which could indeed foster these conditions and orientations were, first of all, some of the agencies of socialization developed by the colonial centers.[57]

Large parts of the educational system under colonialism, with its strong elitist bias which tended to emphasize the idea of trusteeship, as well as with its emphasis on separation from the 'natives' could indeed often serve as one such mechanism of continuity of such orientations; although at the same time this very schooling could also foster some attitude of more universalistic responsibility to legal and administrative frameworks.

Beyond this, the colonial frameworks could also foster broader structural conditions conducive to the perpetuation of patrimonial settings in the very restriction of access to power and resources, which were to a very high degree very closely monopolized by the colonial rulers, as well as by the fostering of more 'segregated' elites within the colonial power framework.

Moreover, the colonial regime, by segregating the access to various types of central resources—those of wealth, central prestige and power—and by controlling power and central prestige as well as all the channels of conversion among them and between them and the more local resources, also tended to perpetuate those conditions.

The colonial and post-colonial settings could also facilitate the development of such orientations and conditions insofar as they tended to undermine the internal solidarity (however weak it might have initially been) of various elites and broader groups alike.

Last, the colonial and post-colonial settings may also reinforce such 'patrimonial' tendencies by the ties of economic, political and cultural dependence on the metropolis which they fostered, all of which minimized the autonomous access of many groups to these resources and increased their dependence on various mediatory distributive agencies.[58]

Truly enough, the various social and national movements, which have developed in these countries and out of which the ruling elites of the new independent states emerged, were initially very strongly opposed, on ideological grounds, to these various tendencies. But such opposition tended to disappear quickly, owing to organizational experience and cultural orientations.

Of special interest is the fact that the patterns of rebellion and outbursts which developed both under colonial rule as well as after independence, showed a close resemblance to those we have found in traditional patrimonial regimes, i.e., their rather other-worldly orientations with strong populistic but few 'reconstructive,' this-wordly, institutional tendencies.[59]

Similarly, many of the heterodox religious movements, especially those which tended to develop after independence, did evince a relatively high degree of 'this-worldly' transformation. Yet most prevalent among them was a transformation into the direction of more 'populist' or collective activities focused around the creation or articulation of new collective symbols, without necessarily giving rise to more 'organized' or disciplined this-worldly activities.

It was only rarely that there developed in some of these movements transformations in the direction creating more 'differentiated,' self-disciplined types of activities and organizations—whether in the political, economic, or educational fields—with a strong motivational orientation in these directions.[60]

But while colonial and post-colonial settings could indeed foster such conditions, they need not always have done so. Here of crucial importance is the degree to which such 'patrimonial' tendencies inherent in the colonial and post-colonial settings are reinforced by the internal orientation of the elites and the major groups. The case of India is of crucial importance from these points of view, in showing how, given other internal orientations and the structure of the traditional society, the neo-patrimonial tendencies, while not absent, did not become predominant.[61]

Thus we see that in the modern ('post-traditional') settings, just as in the traditional ones, it was a combination of predominance of certain types or of 'codes' and orientations, together with certain types of structural conditions that facilitated the crystallization of patrimonial regimes. Both such orientations and structural conditions were similar to those which facilitated the development of such regimes in traditional societies, although here they 'operated' in different sociodemographic, organizational, and cultural ideological settings.

V. THE DYNAMICS OF NEOPATRIMONIAL REGIMES

However great the similarity of the conditions which gave rise to the traditional and modern patrimonial regimes, as well as of the basic characteristics of their political structure and process—and above all the modes of coping with political problems that were prevalent in them—yet, obviously, there were also great differences between the traditional patrimonial and the modern neopatrimonial regimes.

The most important of such differences were, first, those in the political problems which were faced respectively by such traditional and modern regimes, and, second, in close relation to these problems, in the constellations of conditions which could assure the continuity of any specific patrimonial regime. The combined effect of both these differences explains some of the crucial characteristics of the neopatrimonial regimes and of their dynamics.

The major difference in the problems which the modern neopatri-monial regimes faced, as compared with the traditional ones, were due to the prevalence among them of basic premises of modernity analyzed above. All these gave rise to the growth of political demands oriented towards the center and of the quest by those in the center for some continuous support from within the periphery. All these demands have created, as we have seen above, different problems of expansion.

The major dimensions of such expansion were, as we have seen: the establishment and maintenance of some new, broader, unified political framework; the ability of regimes to incorporate new elites within the central political framework, to include new groups and strata into member-ship (whether active or passive) and/or new or different symbolic dimen-sions of collective identity (local, regional, religious); and the ability of regimes to effect possible changes in various new patterns of control over resources and/or their distribution.

This tendency to expansion that was inherent in these regimes, com-bined with growing social differentiation and mobilization, tended also to undermine the continuity of any *specific* structural segregation between different groups and elites, and between the center and periphery that existed in any such regime.

Because of this, in the post-traditional patrimonial regimes—as distinct from the traditional ones—the possibility of development of crises or breakdowns was not something marginal or accidental.

Truly enough, each of these various 'types' (as constructed accord-ing to their respective levels of differentiation and political modernization) of neopatrimonial regimes analyzed above could persist in any given society for a long period of time in some sort of equilibrium with a minimal circulation of its respective elites, insofar as its basic constitutive charac-teristics—i.e., levels of differentiation, political mobilization, as well as the prevalent orientations—did not change greatly.

And yet each such regime was, even if to different degrees, susceptible to the impingement of various new modern types of social and political forces which could undermine whatever uneasy equilibrium was attained within the regime—which could often give rise to various crises, many of which were seemingly common to those which tended to develop in other modern regimes.

But while the possibility of such crises was common to these and other types of modern regimes, the modes of expansion, the relations between different aspects of such expansion, as well as the relation between such expansion and the stability of regimes, varied here greatly from those assumed (in large parts of the social science literature) to be prevalent in the 'classical' modern nation-state and revolutionary regimes.

The models of analysis of these political systems assumed, even if implicitly, that the different dimensions of expansion mentioned above tend to go together, or to develop in some natural sequence, and that the successful expansion of a society in all or most such dimensions of mutual interrelationships is greatly dependent on the stability of its political regime. Moreover, they assumed that there exists a sort of scale-order between, to use Easton's terminology,[62] the stability of the political community, of the regime and of the authorities, and that the expansive capacities of the system, in all dimensions, are greatly dependent on the concurrence of stability of at least both the political community as well as the regime.

Similarly, as is well known, the models of these regimes also assumed certain differences between radicalism and nonradical change—the latter comprising changes in the personal or group composition, without changes in the principles of allocation and distribution of power, and the former implying changes in the very core of such principles; and that the more 'revolutionary' changes of this kind combined also changes of regime with those in principles of distribution of power, in cultural models, as well as in definition of collective symbols and in the criteria of membership in the political and national collectivities.

But these assumptions do not hold in the neopatrimonial regimes. First of all it is rather difficult to point out a 'natural' cycle or trend of development or expansion. It was only, to some degree, with regard to the transition from traditional to nontraditional legitimation and the possibility of continuous development of new social forces raising new demands, that such a trend could be discerned, although in principle, even this trend need not be irreversible.

Beyond these general tendencies, the possibilities of such expansion in the neopatrimonial regimes do not follow a clear developmental pattern which has been assumed to exist in the classic nation-state or revolutionary types of regimes.

Even a brief glance at the historical and contemporary scene will show us that these different dimensions of change in general, and different dimensions of such expansions in particular, need not always go together.[6]

Changes in coalitions of elites could take place with or without incorporation of broader strata into the polity; with or without economic and 'organization' development; with or without changes in the principles of economic distribution of policy, and in center-periphery relations; and each of the latter could also, to some degree at least, vary independently of one another.

Truly enough, one type of such 'resolution' to those situations which were described in the literature as 'breakdowns,' is characterized by a combination of repressive policies in terms of permissiveness to establish autonomous linkages between center and periphery and to develop more active participation of the periphery; by a small degree of the ability to include new elites or to incorporate new groups in the central frameworks, and by regressive and oppressive policies.

Burma and Pakistan, on the one hand, and Argentina on the other, are illustrations of such breakdowns in societies with differing degrees of social mobilization and economic development.

But the comparison between Burma and Pakistan shows that such combinations may be connected with different social orientations of the elites: for example, a seemingly socialist one in Burma and a more 'capitalist' or rightist one in Pakistan. Moreover, the previous period in Pakistan showed that relatively repressive orientations could be connected with a strong developmental bias, and before that relatively repressive orientations were even connected with some attempts (even if limited) of activating the participation of the periphery in 'rural democracies.'

In many other societies repressive and regressive policies could, to some degree, develop independently of each other, and independently of the inclusion of new elites in the center or of the incorporation of new strata in the polity.

Thus, repression and exclusion of a wide range of elites could be coupled, as in Brazil under the military regime, with attempts at economic development and even with attempts at incorporation of wider, but passive, groups into the polity, and at the same time with only minimal changes in the control over resources or the principles of their distribution.[64]

Regressive policies in terms of organizational and economic development could, as in many of the populist regimes of Latin America, be doupled with broadening the scope of participation and incorporation of broader strata into the polity or, as in some Middle Eastern countries (especially Syria and Iraq), they could be connected also with a very large degree of instability in the composition of the central elites.

Indonesia provides some different fascinating variations on these themes. Indonesia, under Sukarno, was based on the incorporation of wider strata into the polity, together with economically regressive regimes. Under Sukarno, there developed, to some degree, a shift to developmental policies connected with a greater limitation and regulation of political participation.

There developed here also a combination of repressive policies giving rise sometimes to extreme measures of expulsion or extermination of 'foreign' groups, coupled with some new distributive extra-active policy by the center which could assure the economic expansion for its own ethnic base and provide a new type of distribution of economic and political power between different ethnic groups.

A similar rather mixed picture emerges here in the relations between stability of regimes and patterns of 'radical' change.

Changes of regimes may or may not be connected with changes in the principles of distribution of power in society; and those in the composition of the ruling group need not always combine also revolutionary changes in the basic cultural model of society.

The possibility of continuity of the cultural model of society can be best seen in the more extreme 'revolutionary' groups, which tended to develop within these regimes. While these could be of several different concrete types—ranging from peasant organization, socialist and syndicalist groups, some of the populist movements, parties and the more recent extremist groups such as student movements and urban guerillas—they still tend to evince some common characteristics. Thus most of these extreme movements tended to develop types of demands which were very much in the pattern of the patrimonial code and can be summarized under three headings: (1) changing the rules of access to the center; (2) broadening the bases of the collectivity whose prestige the center may represent without infusing new orientations of active commitment to the center or changing the attitudes of the broader groups' center to a broader socio-cultural order, or (least of all) changing the low level of commitment to the center; and (3) changing the patterns of distribution of resources. Insofar as these groups approached the center, they tended to oscillate between their desire for immediate and specific rewards and their desire for rather nebulously conceived changing of the overall system. Intense ideological and political conflicts may develop within them that often have little to do with restructuring the center or opening new avenues of participation in it.

The more 'recent' types of such groups, such as the student movements and the guerillas, evince a higher degree of predisposition, together with a high commitment to a revolutionary ideology, but it is still to be seen how much they will, if at all, break with these ideological patterns and orientations.[65]

This does not mean that such changes in the neopatrimonial regimes are random and unsystematic, but only that they tend to develop and coalesce in somewhat different and more complicated ways than those assumed in the models of nation-state and revolutionary regimes. The analysis of these various directions of change of these regimes is still very much before us but some beginning may be attempted by the analysis of the conditions under which they take place.

As in so many other polities in general, and modern polities in particular, these regimes' capacity for expansion is influenced by the elites' degree of internal cohesion; by the degree of internal autonomy and of general openness towards broader and institutional frameworks; by the organizational experience at their disposal; and by the extent of wider attachment to broader political units, as well as the degree of continuity of institutional frameworks.

Thus, economically, socially and politically regressive policies—i.e., those which minimize the expansive capacities of the society—tend to develop in situations characterized by rather weak institutional settings, by the predominance of weak, noncohesive and relatively isolated elites, and by the weakness of more modern groups or elites.

Similarly, the chances for the development of regressive policies is greater in situations or societies in which there exists a high degree of conflict among the major groups in the center, and between them and broader groups. It is also greater in situations characterized by the predominance of relatively isolated and internally not very cohesive elites which may attempt to strengthen their power by populistic appeals, and insofar as such groups are working in the framework of weak institutional settings.

As against this the capacity for expansion is greater insofar as the major elites and strata of any society evince a relatively high degree of internal cohesion, of internal autonomy, and of general openness towards broader and institutional frameworks: insofar as they have some organizational experience at their disposal; and insofar as there exists, within the society, a high degree of attachment to broader political settings, as well as a high degree of continuity of institutional frameworks.

The general conditions which give rise to the broader types of crises or changes are here also similar to those to be found in other types of modern regimes.

Thus, the crises of the narrowest scope tended to develop when there occurred the 'falling out' of groups or cliques within an 'existing' coalition, and when there occurred changes which could give rise through a coup of one sort or another, to some changes in the personal composition of a given restricted elite group, or in the family composition of such cliques. Crises with more far-reaching consequences, i.e., with possible change in the structure of the center or in the distribution of power within it, tend to develop when the structural boiling points of these societies tend to become activated through a combination of conflicts between different elites together with the development of new groups with claims to participate in the center and to change the distribution of power within the society, and especially insofar as such conflicts develop through the competition between more central elites attempting to mobilize the periphery.

But beyond these conditions which are in some degree common to all modern regimes, the severity of such crises of regimes and the types of expansion in the neopatrimonial regimes, are greatly dependent on the combination between these conditions and the possibility of maintaining the different types of segretative arrangements between different groups and sectors, as well as their relatively short-span levels of expectation which we have found to be so crucial for the working of these regimes. Here again only some preliminary indications may be attempted.

Regressive tendencies in general and regressive outcomes of such crises in particular tend to be connected with stability of regimes in situations—such as in many Latin American countries in the 19th century, or in many African countries today—which are characterized by the predominance of relatively weak elites which are segregated from the broader groups in which the conflicts are mostly confined to intra-elite relations and in which context there did not arise great discrepancies between the levels of resources available for immediate distribution and the relatively limited expectations of the broader strata.

Such regressive policies or outcomes tended to be combined with lack of stability of regimes to the degree that such crises (as in the somewh more developed Latin American countries like Ecuador, etc., in the first half of this century, or many Middle Eastern countries) resulted from a combination of conflicts among weak, noncohesive elites within the framework of feeble central institutions together with continuous discrepancies in the levels of expectations of the broader strata and/or with the breakdown of existing segregative arrangements between different (regional, ethnic and status) sectors.

Insofar as the intra or inter 'clique' element is predominant, such crises tend to give rise to a series of continuous political breakdowns and possible stagnation. However, in as much as (for instance, in Indonesia or i Argentina), the discrepancy in the level of expectation and the breakdown of segregative arrangements is more predominant, it may produce more dramatic and 'bloody' cleavages and severe splits which could give rise to more far-reaching changes in regimes and to more repressive policies.

Expansive tendencies or outcomes of crises can be connected (as in Malaysia or the Philippines) with relative stability of regimes since the conflicts which engender them develop between relatively coherent and mutually 'open' elites and groups; they are set within relatively stable and continuous institutions with a tradition of attachment to a common polity. Expansive tendencies can also be connected with relative stability when the demands for expansion do not greatly disrupt the existing segregative arrangements or enable a relatively quick restructuring of some new type of segregative arrangements.

Expansive tendencies tend to be connected with a lack of stability of regimes insofar as the level of conflicts between such groups as in many of the more developed contemporary Latin American societies is relatively high and where there is a tendency not to only break down the existing segregative arrangements, but to polarize the major sectors in the society.

Thus, while in these regimes it is the internal cohesion and solidarity of their respective groups as well as the degree of inter-elite conflicts that is the main variable which influences the degree to which there develop expansive or regressive tendencies within them, it is the combination of these aspects of elite structure with the viability of the existing segregative arrangements that is most decisive in influencing the stability of these regimes.

But what is perhaps even more specific to these regimes is that, as we have already indicated above, it is wrong to talk about 'expansion' or 'regression' of these regimes in general terms which may imply that the different dimensions of expansion necessarily always go together. Indeed the development of such different dimensions of expansion evince here a great variability.

The concrete direction of such changes depends greatly on the relative strength of the central institutional settings, as well as on the balance of power among the contending groups and, above all, on the composition and orientations of the 'winning' or predominant elite.

Among the orientations of the elites, which are of greatest importance from this point of view, are: first the degree to which such elites see themselves as active promoters of social change, and the periphery as potentially active participants in this, or as only an object of the tutelary care of the elite; and second, the relative predominance of 'right' and 'left' orientations of the elites (orientations which have usually been closely related to the social 'class' in whose name the elite purported to rule, and which have affected the different types and principles of redistributive policies) in terms of agrarian reform, redistribution of land or nationalization undertaken by such elites. But these two types of orientations of elites need not always go together, and the (new 'revolutionary') elites need not always be ready to extend the scope of the participation of the periphery in the societal center.

Thus, to give a few illustrations, some of the more specialized (army or technocrat) groups with internal professional solidarity, but with little opening up to other groups and relative segregation from the broader strata, tended often to develop somewhat expansive policies with economic and organizational developmental orientations as well as with some cooptative tendencies, with but little openings for wider participation in the political frameworks.

Some such expansive capacities with regard to more technical and administrative aspects of development, and some expansion of cooptative frameworks, could also be developed by relatively cohesive elites with wider adaptive orientations such as some of the oligarchies of Latin Americ

The more populist leaders, which arise in these societies under the pressure of new social forces, tend to extend the scope of symbolic participation of the population, possibly also to implement some new principles of distribution, but usually with less emphasis on technical development or on actual extension of cooptative frameworks.

The more cohesive such populist elites are and the more they have a tradition of attachment to some broader political community (as for instance in Egypt), the more they are able to assure the maintenance of unified political frameworks, incorporation of new strata into the polity, as well as expansion of some of the cooptative networks, but with little effective overall modernization of organization or economic frameworks or of extension of autonomous participation of wider strata in these political processes.

The greater the differentiation and heterogeneity of such elites, as well as the strength of some tradition of attachment to a unified political framework, and the closer they are also in their segregated activities to the broader strata of their respective societies, the greater also the chances of the opening up of some new center-periphery relations and of effecting changes in the distribution of power within their societies.

Under such conditions changes in the composition of elites and in principles of distribution of power may also be connected with but a minimal disturbance of the regime.

But however great these changes or upheavals, so long as the basic patrimonial codes continued to predominate within the various groups of these societies (and were in one way or another upheld through such structural arrangements as segregation, flow of resources and demands and lack of autonomous access to the center and to its resources), some type of patrimonial regimes were also maintained; although, as we have seen, the various differences among these regimes could indeed greatly influence the intensity of conflicts, the type of political struggle or the degree in which these regimes were able to institutionalize a more continuous capacity of expansion with a smaller degree of conflicts and crises. This could indeed be seen in the basic characteristics analyzed above

58

and in the radical movements which tended to develop in these societies.

The possibilities of some more 'radical' changes in some of the aspects of the political codes could develop in two ways. One is through the development of a rather strong revolutionary elite, with at least some new 'codes' or orientations and some responsiveness to them among the broader strata. However, the degree to which such an elite could be successful in implementing changes may depend greatly on the relative strength of such an elite in relation to other elites, as well as on the extent to which it no longer shares all the elements of the patrimonial code. Insofar as both conditions tend to develop, then, as perhaps in Cuba, Mexico or Turkey, they may indeed give rise to some far-reaching changes in the basic orientation of the political system, even if some of the patrimonial orientations, such as the strong emphasis on the distributive and guardianship roles of the state, tend to remain. Otherwise it may indeed provide yet another case of intensive crises, and may often give rise to at least a momentary, and sometimes more prolonged regression.

The second possibility of changing at least some of the basic patrimonial orientations could take place, in principle, through various structural changes, and especially through the combination of the breakdown of the segregation between different groups and between the flow of different types of resources and the development of a more autonomous access of major groups and strata to the sources of power.

Some such developments may perhaps be happening in the Philippines, or perhaps in Venezuela, but these are as yet developments too new and halting to be evaluated at this stage.

Here indeed of great interest is the problem as to whether the very patrimonial nature of these regimes limits the possibility of far-reaching changes in displacement of elites and in the distribution of power within them. i.e., of what is usually called 'revolutionary' change; or, in other words, whether any such 'real' 'revolutionary' change can take place only in the framework of a nation-state, of a 'revolutionary class' in a modern society; or whether even when such revolutionary change takes place these regimes still may retain many of their patrimonial characteristics.

It is too early at this time to give any final judgement on these problems, but the recent developments in Chile, on the one hand, and in Cuba on the other, may throw some light on their classification.

VI. SUMMARY AND THEORETICAL CONCLUSIONS

In the preceding chapters we have attempted to answer the question posed at the beginning of our analysis, namely, whether there can be any justification for the use of the term 'patrimonial'—a term derived from the analysis of traditional, historical political systems—to the analysis of more modern ones.

We have found that such use could indeed be very fruitful, but only insofar as the term 'patrimonial' is used to designate not a level of 'development' or differentiation of political regimes, but rather a specific way of coping with the major problem of political life which may cut across different levels of 'development' or structural complexity.

It was the use of this term which enabled us to identify those characteristics which traditional and modern patrimonial regimes share, as well as the differences between them, and also to point out the differences between ('traditional') patrimonial and other traditional regimes, such as Empires, and between modern neopatrimonial ones and others—e.g., 'nation-state' or 'revolutionary' modern regimes.

The most important common characteristics of traditional and modern patrimonial regimes are: the basic modes of coping with political problems; the relations between center and periphery; the major types of policies developed by their rulers; and the general format of political struggle and process.

The common characteristics of traditional and modern political regimes are at least partially explained by some condition of their emergence, by the nature, composition and internal solidarity of the major groups and elites, and by the basic codes or orientations prevalent within these groups. It is such groups and elites with such orientations that tend to develop those types or patterns of activity and organization which give rise to the crystallization of patrimonial regimes, and they also tend to develop policies which can assure that the interaction between such groups and between the center and periphery will facilitate the continuity of their regimes.

But the continuity of such conditions is not ever fully given or assured and every single regime of this type is always prone to the possibility of acute crises and of its demise. It is here that some of the major differences between the traditional and the modern patrimonial regimes stand out.

The major differences between the traditional and modern patrimonial regimes are to be found, first, in the types of problems and demands with which they have to cope; problems and demands which are derived from different levels of social differentiation and mobilization and from basic sociocultural and political premises. Second, and closely related to these are also the differences in the patterns of political organization, ranging from cliques and kingly household in the traditional sphere to more complex, bureaucratic or party organizations in the modern ones.

But beyond everything they vary with respect to the conditions of their stability. It is not that the modern patrimonial regimes are necessarily more volatile or unstable than the traditional ones, but rather that, as in all modern regimes, there develops a continuous tendency to change and expansion. But just as the traditional patrimonial regime differs from other traditional-Imperial or city state regimes—both in the various patterns of political organization analyzed above, and in their patterns of change—so do also the neopatrimonial ones differ from other types of modern nation-state, revolutionary, Japanese or Indian models.

They differ with regard to: the ways in which they cope with their 'cultural' (symbolic) and organizational problems; with regard to post-traditional societies and the specific types of conflicts to which they are especially sensitive; the types of conditions under which the potentialities for such conflicts become articulated into more specific boiling points, which may threaten the stability of these regimes; the ways in which the regimes cope with these problems and conflicts; and especially with regard to the ways of incorporating various types of political demands in general and those for growing participation in the political order in particular. These models also vary with regard to the degree of coalescence of boundaries of different systems and collectivities, e.g., political, cultural, ethnic, and of their respective symbols; and they vary in the different degree of continuity of such different symbols in face of changing levels of structural differentiation and change of regimes.

The major points of the preceding summary have some closely related general theoretical implications. Our analysis indicates that the populations which live within the confines of what usually has been designated as a 'society,' or of a macro-societal order, are not usually organized in one 'system,' but rather in several different ways and on several levels; that these different levels of organizations of social activities may be carried by different parts of the populations within different structures; that these structures evince different patterns of organization, continuity and change; and that these structures and patterns may change within the 'same' society to different degrees or in different ways in various areas of social life (although they are not, of course, unconnected).

The preceding analysis has indicated both some of the more important distinctions between such different aspects or levels of organization of social life as well as some of the ways in which they are systematically interconnected. It has indicated that among the distinctions current in sociological literature, of special importance, from the point of view of comparative macro-sociological analysis and the analysis of social change, are those among, first, different collectivities and organizations, organized as 'systems' or congeries of 'systems' with their various respective boundary-maintaining mechanisms; second, broader collectivities, communities and/or sociocultural orders which are not necessarily structured as organizations, but which are focused around various symbols of collective identity; third, different levels of structural differentiation of social activities; and last, the cultural orientations and the various 'codes' analyzed above.

All these aspects or levels of social order organize the conversion of basic social resources in certain basic institutional frameworks and patterns, i.e., 'economic,' 'political,' etc., which have been analyzed fully in sociological literature, and which can be organized in different organizational patterns. But each of these aspects of social order 'organizes' the conversion of resources through social activities from a distinct point of view and in a distinct pattern and evinces also different patterns of continuity or change.[66]

The major loci of 'organization-systemic' stability or change of social activities are those collectivities which are structured as organizations or sets of organizations—of which political systems and regimes, as well as different organizational substructures (family, workshops, formal organizations, etc.) are the best illustrations.

Such a system faces, as is well known by now, a series of problems derived from the interaction of these collectivities with its external and internal environments. These problems have been designated in various ways in sociological literature, the best known of which has been the Parsonian classification into adaptive, integrative goal-oriented and pattern maintenance ones.

These problems impinge on each such collectivity through the demands of its members or sub-units for resources, for access to positions, for participation in its centers, and through the external pressures and needs for resources and services from outside of its systemic boundaries.

All such collectivities and organizations evince, in face of both external and internal impingements and of the relations between these two, some combination of homeostatic tendencies together with tendencies to extend their boundaries, i.e., both to adapt to a given environment—in itself probably created to a large degree by some preceding social creativity—as well as to extend such environment, to create a new environment.

Out of the interaction between these tendencies of such systems and the ways in which they cope with their internal and external problems, there develops, as has been so often stressed in the literature, in each such 'system' or organization a specific pattern of division of labor and of allocation of power and resources and control over them, of control of access to the major positions within the system and of the setting of its specific systemic boundaries which differentiate it from other organizations or from other aspects of its environment.[67]

The continuity of each such collectivity, organization, or sets of organizations, is contingent on a certain dynamic equilibrium among:

(a) the resources at the disposal of individuals and groups within it; (b) the private goals of individuals or of the 'subgroups'; (c) the collective goals of the collectivity; (d) the resources needed for the implementation of these goals and for the maintenance of the boundaries of the collectivity and organization.

This dynamic equilibrium may always be undermined through various processes of change and through the impingement of internal and external forces alike. Such processes of change 'release' the various resources available for social activities from the existing organized patterns and from boundaries of the given systems; they give rise to the different concrete constellations of the general problems which these collectivities 'face,' and may enable the development, in all institutional spheres, of new organizational resources which can be mobilized for the solution of these problems.

A second aspect of social order or a second level of organization of social activities and conversion of resources is to be found in collectivities, communities or sociocultural orders such as kinship, ethnic relations, cultural orders, as well as to some degree hierarchical strata—whose systemic boundaries are organized or patterned around symbols or likeness of common attributes and of participation in them, but which are not necessarily structured as systems with clear organizational boundaries—although they may very often at least partially coincide with some organizational structures, i.e., with political regimes.

The major mechanisms through which these collectivities or orders function are those which regulate the specifications of the major attributes which define the 'likeness' or 'similarity' according to which the boundaries of the respective orders are set up; of the rights and limitation of access to such attributes and the consequent participation in the respective order or collectivity; of the range of conditional and unconditional obligations and rights accruing through membership in such collectivities or orders; and of the consequent terms of conditional and unconditional access to the various resources and positions which are available according to such criteria.[68]

The pattern of relations established within any such collectivity or order, its specific type of dynamic equilibrium, may be challenged or undermined especially: by groups or individuals who want to propagate different attributes of 'likeness' or 'similarity' as the major definitions of the boundaries of the collectivity or order; by the demands from nonmembers to access to membership; by demands for changing the rules and access and the patterns of obligations accruing from them.

Beyond the homeostatic or expansive tendencies or problems of relatively well organized social systems, as well as the organization of symbolic definition of the level of boundaries of collectivities and of social and cultural orders, an additional way in which social conversion of resources in social interaction is organized, and which has been especially stressed in our analysis, is that which focuses around what has been called 'codes,' or cultural orientations with definite structural derivatives.

These codes or orientations provide directives or choices with respect to some of the perennial problems immanent in the nature of human life in social and cultural context, and especially they provide:

(a) the major ways of looking at the problems of human existence and of social and cultural order, of posing the major questions about them, especially around such problems as: the definition of the relative importance of different dimensions of human existence and their bearing on the definition of cultural and political identity; the perception of the interrelation and mutual relevance of the cosmic, the cultural, the social and the political orders; the patterns of participation in the formation of social and cultural orders; and the bases of legitimation of such orders;

(b) the symbolic and organizational answers to these problems; and

(c) the organization of various institutional and symbolic structures for the implementation of different types of solutions or answers to these problems.[69]

Thus, in a way, these codes address themselves to problems which are different from the more structural-systemic problems of organized collectivities or from those which are related to the setting up of the boundaries of social and cultural order.

But at the same time these codes are not only some general, broad, cultural orientations or general value orientations. They are much closer to what Weber has called 'Wirtschaftsethik,' i.e., to general modes of 'religious' or 'ethical' orientations to a specific institutional sphere and its problems: the evaluation of this sphere in terms of the premises of a given religion or tradition about the basic problems of the cosmic order and of their relations to human and social existence, and the consequent structural and behavioral derivatives of such evaluation.

Or, in a somewhat different paraphrase, such 'Ethik' or 'codes' connote a general mode of orientation towards the symbolic and organizational aspects of a given sphere of social life. Thus such a mode, in a sense, goes beyond concrete comments and structures, but, at the same time, may guide the crystallization of greatly varying and changing types of cultural contents and orgnizational structures.

Our analysis has shown that unlike what has often been assumed in sociological literature, there need not be—perhaps there cannot be—a full convergence or congruence in any 'population' or 'society' between the broader organizational systems and those of the different sociocultural orders, and different 'societies' may vary greatly with respect to the degree of such congruence. Moreover, there need not also exist a convergence between the boundaries of the different cultural, ethnic, religious or hierarchical orders; between their respective symbols of collective identity or an identity in the rules which govern the access to membership in these collectivities, their duties and obligations.

Similarly it need not be assumed that change, for whatever reasons— in the levels of structural differentiation or complexity within any group or population—does necessarily lead to one type of concomitant change in the definition of symbols of collectivity and their boundaries, in the nature of the respective regimes, or in the allocation of power within them.

Similarly the various codes, their various constellations, and above all their structural derivatives, may cut across different levels of social differentiation; across changes of regimes, of boundaries, of collectivities, of identities and symbols of collective identity. Thus such codes and their structural derivatives constitute foci of similarity or continuity, or possible discontinuity—in the same 'society' in different stages or periods of its history—but of a continuity or similarity of stability or change of a different kind from that which characterizes the different types of boundary-maintaining systemic units or boundaries of collective identities.

What has perhaps been of special interest in the analysis of traditional patrimonial and of neopatrimonial regimes has been the possible similarity or continuity of such codes and of their structural derivatives across changes in the levels of differentiation in the boundaries of collective identity, types of regime in different historical periods of the 'same' society.

At the same time these codes differ also from the immanent, 'contents-directed' structures of different symbolic realms as well as from the more or less articulated symbolic models of society, of social and cultural order, which are prevalent within a 'society.'

Truly enough, the expression of these codes is, of course, always couched in symbolic terms and very often their fullest articulation can be found in organized and articulated cultural systems or artifacts—be they philosophic, theological or architectural ones.

But the internal structure of any such constellation of 'codes' which may be prevalent within a society is not identical with that of such 'intellectual' creations in terms of their own 'logical' dynamics and premises.

Whatever systemic or 'structural' characteristics these codes or their constellations evince are not articulated in terms of purely intellectual models but in the juxtaposition of their orientations to different problems: those inherent in the systemic problems of social organization and in the givens of sociocultural life and existence.

Hence different codes or constellations of such codes may be operative 'beneath' similarly-looking cultural creations or 'symbolic' 'ideal' expressions of the proper social and cultural order—whether or not they are those expressed in the orthodoxies or heterodoxies of a given culture.[70]

Our analysis does not indicate that—unlike what has been sometimes assumed in those parts of the literature which have dealt with the relation between relations, 'values' or 'cultures,' and the structural prerequisites of social systems—however distinct these various aspects of social order are from one another, their structural derivatives have specific and systematic connections. Our analysis also indicates that the various codes not only greatly influence the various discrete organizational aspects of these societies, such as the structure of political process or several asepcts of hierarchical organization which were analyzed above, but also greatly influence much more 'basic' aspects of the working of the social systems within which they are predominant.

First, as these various codes and constellations of codes influence the range of 'permissible' questions and answers about some of the basic problems of social and cultural centers, they set up some of the parameters and boundaries of the internal and external environments of the respective 'societies' or systems.

They are very influential in defining the environment within which the organizational problems of such systems are set. They either influence the concrete responses to the range of different possibilities which the organizational exigencies open up at any given or historical situation, or at any level of social differentiation; or, through changes in the goals of collectivities, they help in the creation of the new sociocultural environment, thus potentially changing the range of such organizational possibilities and of the boundaries of collectivities.

In this way they influence the range of systemic sensitivity of such systems: the ranges of conflicts and crises which may tend to develop within them, the salience of such different potential conflicts for the continuity of the given system; the working of its central integrative mechanisms and especially the ways in which the structuring of flow of resources in a society, (i.e., segregated or cross-cutting ways) affects those mechanisms; the ways in which different sytems cope with the specific range of problems and crises which they face, as well as the possible outcome of such crises—especially the modes of 'incorporation' or of various dimensions of social and political expansion.

Similarly, our analysis indicates some of the meeting points between the crystallization of codes and their structural derivatives and the more articulated intellectual creation, and/or models of social and cultural life of society and of social and cosmic order, which are present in societies. As has been abundantly shown in existing literature, such models may provide ritual expression of the contradictions which are inherent in the continuous juxtaposition between the problem of social existence and the exigencies of structural division of labour and allocation of power in a society; thus they provide articulation of pattern of motivation to social action and of its pattern of legitimation. Such articulation takes place most fully in ritual situations or in movements of heterodoxy and rebellion.[71]

The nature and importance of the meeting points between the various aspects of social order analyzed above stands out more clearly if we attempt to see their implications for comparative macro-sociological analysis in general and for analysis of change in particular, especially of the ways in which, within each 'type' of society—as constructed according to the different levels of structural differentiation of free-floating resources or of cultural contents—there may develop, although certainly not limitless, a great variety of different models of social and cultural orders.

As is well known, some of the major differences between different types of societies—different types of 'traditional' societies such as 'archaic,' 'historical,' etc.—and between traditional and modern ones (or any other similar types) have usually been, in sociological literature, constructed according to criteria of structural differentiation or according to the contents of different cultural symbols or spheres, and present in a rather taxonomic way.[72]

Bur while these asepcts are obviously of great interest for macro-sociological comparisions, our analysis seems to indicate that perhaps the most important aspect of such different levels of differentiation is that they point out the nature of the constellations of forces which are generated from within the internal and external environments of any society, which impinge on these collectivities or systems, and which create various concrete problems for them, as well as provide various (old and new) types of resources through which such problems can be coped with.

But in such situations of change there develops not just one possibility of the restructuring of such resources and activities, in the direction of new levels of differentiation, but rather a great variety of such possibilities.[73] Different societies within each such type in general, and among modern and modernizing societies (and in principle in any other 'type'), differ not only, as was so often assumed for instance in the literature on modernization, in the degree of structural development. They differ also, as has become more and more apparent in research and as has been shown in our analysis of patrimonialism, in the ways in which their basic problems are perceived and coped with; and these are, as we have seen in our preceding analysis, greatly influenced by the different constellations of codes which are prevalent in these societies. Within each such 'type' (traditional or modern, etc.) of society there developed different models of social and political order which define different parameters of traditionality or of modernity: such as, for instance, patrimonial or different ('religious,' 'military') Imperial regimes in traditional societies, or such as the 'neopatrimonial,' 'nation-state,' or 'revolutionary class' models among modern societies.

These different models vary: with regard to the ways in which they cope with their 'cultural' (symbolic) and organizational problems; with regard to the ways in which they incorporate various demands for expansion in general, and the combinations of different dimensions of expansion, in particular; in the relation between stability of regimes and of their expansive or regressive tendencies; in the degree of coalescence of boundaries of different systems and collectivities (e.g., political, cultural, ethnic) and of their respective symbols; and in different degrees of continuity of such different symbols in face of changing levels of structural differentiation and change of regimes.

It is here also that some of the similarities between different societies cutting across levels of differentiation, systemic and collective boundaries, tend to arise, thus pointing to a more variegated approach to comparative analysis.

Obviously, all these considerations open up a series of new problems for sociological analysis: who are the carriers and mechanisms of the different aspects of social order analyzed above, and what are the relations between them; of the structural conditions which facilitate the development of different types of codes and the continuous maintenance of their major structural derivatives; of the conditions under which such codes may change or shifts in the relative importance of different codes within a society may take place; and as to whether the 'transition' from one type of society to another (e.g., from a 'traditional' to a modern one) is dependent on change in the existing constellation of codes or is it possible to envisage such transitions just through changes in cultural contents or through structural differentiation? The further investigation of all these problems seems to us to be of great importance for the analysis of social change.

NOTES

1. See Guenther Roth, "Personal rulership, patrimonialism and empire-building in the new state," World Politics, Vol. XX, No. 2 (Jan. 1968); and A. R. Zolberg, *Creating Political Order: The Party States of West Africa* (Chicago: Rand McNally, 1966).

2. E. Gellner, "The great patron: a reinterpretation of tribal rebellions," Archives Européens de Sociologie, Tome X, No. 1 (1969), pp. 61, 70; and John Waterbury, *The Commander of the Faithful: The Moroccan Elite* (London: Weidenfeld and Nicholson, 1970).

3. See Clifford Geertz, "Primordial sentiments and civil policies in the new states," in Geertz (ed.), *Old Societies and New States* (Chicago: University of Chicago Press, 1963); and Geertz, *The Religion of Java* (New York: Free Press, 1969).

4. See Fred W. Riggs, "Agraria and industria: toward a typology of comparative administration," in W. J. Sifflin (ed.), *Toward a Comparative Study of Public Administration in Developing Countries* (Boston: Houghton Mifflin, 1964), pp. 241-312.

5. See S. N. Eisenstadt, "General introduction: the scope and problems of political sociology," in Eisenstadt (ed.), *Political Sociology* (New York: Basic Books, 1971).

For some of the criticism of the original paradigm of modernization see: A. A. Mazrui, "From social Darwinism to current theories of modernization," World Politics, Vol. XXI, No. 1 (Oct. 1968), pp. 69-83; C. S. Whitaker, Jr., "A dysrhythmic process of political change," World Politics, Vol. XIX, No. 2 (Jan. 1967), pp. 190-217; Joseph R. Gusfield (ed.), "Tradition and modernity: conflict and congruence," Journal of Social Issues, Vol. XXIV, No. 4 (Oct. 1968); R. N. Bellah (ed.), *Religion and Progress in Modern Asia* (New York: The Free Press, 1965), especially Soedjatmoko, "Cultural motivations to progress: the 'exterior' and 'interior' views," pp. 1-14, and Clifford Geertz, "Modernization in a Muslim society," pp. 93-108; A. R. Desai (ed.), *Essays on Modernization of Underdeveloped Societies* (Bombay: Thacker, 1971), Vol. I, especially Robert Sinai, "Modernization and the poverty of the social sciences," pp. 53-75, W. F. Wertheim, "The way toward modernity," pp. 76-94, and A. R Desai, "Need for revaluation of the concept," pp. 458-474; Gino Germani, "Stages of modernization," International Journal, Vol. XXIV, No. 3 (summer 1969), pp. 463-448; S. N. Eisenstadt, "Reflections on a theory of modernization" in Arnold Rivkin (ed.), *Nations by Design: Institution-Building in Africa* (Garden City, N.Y.: Anchor Books, 1968), pp. 35-61; and Eisenstadt, "Some new looks at the problem of relations between traditional societies and modernization," Economic Development and Cultural Change, Vol. XVI, No. 3 (April 1968), pp. 436-449.

6. On these concepts see S. N. Eisenstadt, "Breakdowns of modernization," Economic Development and Cultural Change, Vol. XII, No. 4 (July 1964), pp. 345-367; and S. P. Huntington, "Political development and political decay," World Politics, Vol. XVII, No. 3 (April 1965), pp. 367-388.

7. Riggs' 'sala' model, which does attempt to look at these societies as self-sustaining, does not on the whole view them as such transitional types. For illustrations of some of the vicissitudes of the concept of 'traditional societies' and 'transitional societies' see: Marion Levy, *Modernization and the Structure of Societies* (Princeton, N.J.: Princeton University Press, 1966); Frank X. Sutton, "Social theory and comparative politics," in Harry Eckstein and David Apter (eds.), *Comparative Politics: A Reader* (New York: The Free Press, 1963), 67 ff; Cyril E. Black, *The Dynamics of Modernization* (New York: Harper & Row, 1966), p. 7;

Dankwart A. Rustow, *A World of Nations* (Washington: Brookings Institution, 1967), p. 3; Dankwart A. Rustow and Robert E. Ward, "Introduction" in Ward and Rustow (eds.), *Political Modernization in Japan and Turkey* (Princeton: Princeton University Press, 1964), pp. 6-7; Reinhard Bendix, "Tradition and modernity reconsidered," Comparative Studies in Society and History, Vol. IX, No. 3 (April 1967), pp. 292-293 Daniel Lerner, *The Passing of Traditional Society* (New York: The Free Press, 1958), p. 438; Joseph R. Gusfield, "Tradition and modernity: misplaced polarities in the study of social change," American Journal of Sociology, Vol. LXXII (Jan. 1966), pp. 351-362; Gusfield, "Tradition and modernity: conflict and congruence," loc. cit.; and Hideo Kishimoto, "Modernization versus westernization in the East," Cahiers d'Histoire Mondiale, VII (1963), pp. 871-874.

8. Some analyses of the colonial situation can be found in: J. S. Furnivall, *Colonial Policy and Practice: A Comparative Study of Burma and Netherlands India* (Cambridge, Eng.: Cambridge University Press, 1948 and New York: New York University Press, 1956); S. N. Eisenstadt, *Essays on Social and Political Aspects of Economic Development* (The Hague: Mouton, 1958); and Immanuel M. Wallerstein (ed.), *Social Change, The Colonial Situation* (New York: Wiley & Sons, 1969). For a recent study of one area, see Y. Turner (ed.), *Colonization in Africa, 1870-1960* (Cambridge, Eng.: Cambridge University Press, 1971).

9. See, for instance: Max Weber, "Gerontocracy, patriarchalism and patrimonial authority," in Max Weber (ed.), *The Theory of Social and Economic Organization,* trans. by Talcott Parsons and A. M. Henderson (New York: Oxford University Press, 1947), pp. 346-365; and William Delany, "The development and decline of patrimonial and bureaucratic administrations," Administrative Science Quarterly, Vol. VII, No. 4 (March 1963), pp. 458-501.

10. See Roth, op. cit.; and Zolberg, op. cit.

11. Gellner, op. cit.; Geertz, *Religion of Java,* op. cit.; and Waterbury, op. cit.

12. On the general political history of these societies, see: David Joel Steinberg (ed.), *In Search of Southeast Asia* (New York: Praeger, 1971); W. F. Wertheim, "Southeast Asia," International Encyclopedia of the Social Sciences, Vol. I, pp. 423-428; John Bastin and Henry J. Benda, *A History of Modern Southeast Asia* (Englewood Cliffs, N. J.: Prentice Hall, 1963); John Bastin (ed.), *The Emergence of Modern Southeast Asia: 1511-1957* (Englewood Cliffs, N. J.: Prentice Hall, 1967); Robert O. Tilman (ed.), *Man, State and Society in Contemporary Southeast Asia* (New York: Praeger, 1969); and Victor Purcell, *The Chinese in Southeast Asia* (London, New York: Oxford University Press, 1951).

On Thailand, see: Herbert Phillips, *Thai Peasant Personality* (Berkeley: University of California Press, 1965); Kenneth Wells, *Thai Buddhism: Its Rites and Activities* (Bangkok: The Bangkok Times Press, 1939); Horace Geoffrey Quaritch Wales, *Ancient Siamese Government and Administration* (London: B. Quaritch, 1934); and Robert Lingat, "La Double crise de l'église bouddhique au Siam, 1767-1851," Journal of World History, Vol. IV, No. 2 (1958), pp. 402-425.

On Burma, see: John F. Cady, *A History of Modern Burma* (Ithaca, N.Y.: Cornell University Press, 1969); and Furnivall, op. cit.

On Indonesia, see: George McT. Kahin, *Nationalism and Revolution in Indonesia* (Ithaca, N.Y.: Cornell University Press, 1962); and J. D. Legge, *Indonesia* (Englewood Cliffs, N.J.: Prentice Hall, 1964).

On the Philippines, see: Fred Eggan, Evett Hester and Norton Ginsburg (eds.), *Area Handbook on the Philippines* (Chicago: University of Chicago for the H.R.A.F., 1965

Mario D. Azmora (ed.), *Studies in Philippine Anthropology in Honor of H. Otley Beyer* (Quezon City: Alemar-Pheonix, 1967).

On Ceylon, see Sidney A. Pakeman, *Ceylon* (London: Been, 1964).

On Malasia, see Wang Gungwu (ed.), *Malaysia* (New York: Praeger, 1964).
     13. For more detail, see the literature cited in note 12 above.
     14. On some of the general characteristics of the economic process in these countries see Benjamin Rivlin and Joseph S. Szyliowicz (eds.), *The Contemporary Middle East: Traditions and Innovations* (New York: Random House, 1965), esp. United Nations Report, "Changing socio-economic patterns in the Middle East," pp. 299-313; C.A.O. Van Nieuwenhuijze, "The Near Eastern village: A Profile," pp. 314-324; "International labor organization report, employment prospects of children and young people in the Near and Middle East," pp. 359-367; Norman Burns, "Planning economic development in the Arab world," pp. 368-374; and Robert B. Pettengill, "Population control to accelerate economic progress in the Middle East," pp. 375-387.

On Southeast Asia, see: Frank Goaly, et. al., (eds.), *Underdevelopment and Economic Nationalism in Southeast Asia* (Ithaca, N.Y.: Cornell University Press, 1969); J.A.C. Mackie, *Problems of the Indonesian Inflation* (Ithaca, N.Y.: Southeast Asia Program, Dept. of Asian Studies, Cornell University, 1967); Hans Schmidt, "Post-colonial politics: a suggested interpretation of the Indonesian experience, 1950-58," Australian Journal of Politics and History, Vol. IX, No. 2 (Nov. 1963); Soedjatmoko, *Economic Development as a Cultural Problem* (Ithaca, N.Y.: Southeast Asia Program, Dept. of Asian Studies, Cornell Unversity, 1968); John Adams and Harvy Hancock, "Land & economy in traditional Vietnam," Journal of Southeast Asian Studies, Vol. I, No. 2 (Sept. 1970) pp. 90-98; Frank H. Golay, *The Philippines: Public Policy and National Economics* (Ithaca, N.Y.: Cornell University Press, 1961); James J. Puthucheary, *Ownership and Control of the Malay Economy* (Singapore: D. Moore for Eastern Universities Press, 1969); C. K. Meed, *Land Law and Custom in the Colonies* (London: G. Cumberledge, Oxford University Press, 1964); and Thomas H. Silcock (ed.), *Readings in Malayan Economics* (Singapore: D. Moore for Eastern Universities Press, 1961).

     15. On the general trends of political development in these societies, see the literature cited in note 12 above, as well as Roger Scott, *The Politics of New States* (London: Allen & Unwin, 1970).

On Asia in general, see: Saul Rose, "Political modernization in Asia," France-Asie/Asia, Vol. XXII, No. 1, No 192 (1st quarter, 1968), pp. 31-45; Richard L. Park, "Second thoughts on Asian democracy," Asian Survey, Vol. I, No. 2 (April, 1961), pp. 28-31; and Rupert Emerson, *From Empire to Nation: The Rise to Self-Assertion of Asian and African Peoples* (Cambridge, Mass.: Harvard University Press, 1960).

On Pakistan: H. J. Friedman, "Notes on Pakistan's basic democracies," Asian Survey. Vol. I, No. 10 (Dec. 1961), pp. 19-24; H. J. Friedman, "Pakistan's experiment in basic democracies," Pacific Affairs, Vol. XXXIII, No. 2 (June, 1960), pp. 107-125; and R. L. Mellena, "The basic democracies system in Pakistan," Asian Survey, Vol. I, No. 6 (Aug. 1961), pp. 10-15.

On the Middle East: Khalid bin Sayeed, "Collapse of parliamentary democracy in Pakistan," The Middle East Journal, Vol. XII, No. 4 (Autumn, 1959), pp. 389-406; Rivlin and Szyliowicz (eds.), op. cit., esp. Richard H. Pfaff, "Disengagement from traditionalism in Turkey and Iran," pp. 417-427; Morroe Berger, "Pre-populist and Populist regimes," pp. 428-432; Elie Salem, "Emerging government in the Arab world," pp. 440-451; Mohammed Shafi Agwani, "The Ba'th: a study in contemporary Arab politics," pp. 452-460; and Joseph S. Szyliowicz, "Political dynamics of rural Turkey," pp. 489-500; Majid Khadluri, "The coup d'etat of 1936," Middle East Journal, Vol. II, (1948), pp. 270-292; and Alrod Carleton, "The Syrian coups d'etat of 1949," Middle East Journal, Vol. IV (1950), pp. 1-11.

On Southeast Asia: Saul Rose (ed.), *Politics in Southern Asia* (London: MacMillan; New York: St. Martin's Press, 1963); Lauriston Sharp, "Colonial regimes in Southeast Asia," Far Eastern Survey, Vol. XV (1946), pp. 49-53; Saul Rose, *Socialism in Southern Asia* (London, New York: Oxford University Press, 1959); Guy J. Pauker, "Political doctrines and practical politics in Southeast Asia," Pacific Affairs, Vol. XXXV, No. 1 (Spring 1962), pp. 3-11; and L. H. Palmier, "Sukarno: the nationalist," Pacific Affairs, Vol. XXX, No. 2., (July 1957), pp. 101-120.

On Indonesia: Harry J. Benda, "Decolonization in Indonesia: the problem of continuity and change," American Historical Review, Vol. LXX, No. 4 (July 1965), pp. 1058-73; J. M. Van der Kroef, "The changing pattern of Indonesia's representative government," Canadian Journal of Economics and Political Science, Vol. XXVI, No. 2 (May 1960), pp. 215-240; "Economic reconstruction and the struggle for political power in Indonesia," The World Today, Vol. XV, No. 3 (March 1959), pp. 105-114; (signed S.S.). J. M. Van der Kroef, "New political patterns in Indonesia," The World Today, Vol. XXV, No. 5 (May 1969), pp. 219-230; L. H. Palmier, "Centralization in Indonesia; review article," Pacific Affairs, Vol. XXXIII, No. 2 (June 1960), pp. 169-180; Tarzie Vittachi, *The Fall of Sukarno* (New York: Praeger, 1967); and Walter Schilling, "Der sturz Sukarnos und die 'neue ordnung' in Indonesien Politische Studien, 21 Jahrgang (March-April 1970), pp. 172-184.

On Burma: J. H. Badgley, "Burma's political crisis," Pacific Affairs, Vol. XXX, No. 4, (Dec. 1958), pp. 336-352; Edmund R. Leach, *Political Systems of Highland Burma*, 2nd ed. (London: London School of Economics, 1964; Boston: Beacon Press, 1967); J. S. Furnivall, *The Governance of Modern Burma* (New York: International Secretariat, Institute of Pacific Relations, 1958; 2nd ed. enl., 1960); J. H. Badgley, "Burma the nexus of socialism and two political traditions," Asian Survey, Vol. VI, No. 2 (Feb. 1963), pp. 89-96; and F. N. Trager, "Political divorce in Burma," Foreign Affairs, Vol. XXXVII, No. 2 (Jan. 1959), pp. 317-327.

On Vietnam: Roger Scott, op. cit.; John McAlister and Paul Mus, "The Vietnamese and their revolution" (New York: The Center of International Studies, Princeton University, 1970); Dennis J. Duncanson, "Vietnam as a nation-state," Modern Asian Studies, Vol. III, No. 2 (1969); and R. C. Scigliano, "The electoral process in South Vietnam: politics in an under-developed state," Midwest Journal of Political Science, Vol. IV, No. 2 (May 1960), pp. 138-161.

On Thailand: Lucien M. Hanks, Jr., "Merit and power in the Thai social order," American Anthropologist, Vol. LXIV, No. 6 (Dec. 1962), pp. 1247-61; Prince Dhani Nivat, "The reconstruction of King Rama I of the Chakri dynasty," Journal of the Siam Society, Vol. XLIII, No. 1 (1955), pp. 21-47; Akin Rabibhadana, *The Organization of Thai Society in the Early Bangkok Period, 1782-1873* (Ithaca, N.Y.: Cornell University Press, 1969); and David K. Wyatt, "Family politics in nineteenth century Thailand," Journal of Southeast Asian History, Vol. IX, No. 2 (1969), pp. 208-228.

On Malaya: John M. Gullick, *Indigenous Political Systems of Western Malaya* (Londo University of London, Athlone Press, 1958); K. J. Ratnam, "Religion and politics in

Malaya," in Tilman (ed.), op. cit.; K. J. Ratnam, *Communalism and the Political Process in Malaya* (Kuala Lumpur: University of Malaya Press, 1965); and R. S. Milne, "Political modernization in Malaysia," Journal of Commonwealth Political Studies, Vol. VII, No. 1 (March 1969), pp. 3-20.

On the Philippines: Jean Grossholtz, *Politics in the Philippines* (Boston and Toronto: Little Brown & Co. 1964); and Jose' Veloso Abueva, "Administrative culture and behavior and middle civil servants in the Philippines," in Edward W. Weidner (ed.), *Development Administration in Asia* (Durham, N.C.: Duke University Press, 1970), pp. 132-186.

On Latin America: Russell H. Fitzgibbon, "Dictatorship and democracy in Latin America," International Affairs, Vol. XXXVI, No. 1 (Jan. 1960); Jacques J. Dumont, "Le conflit 'socie'tal' et le processus de changment politique et economique. Le cas de la 'violenua' et Colombie," (premier partie), Civilizatione. Vol. XVI, No. 2 (1966), pp. 173-185; and Maurice Zeitlin and James Petras, "The working class vote in Chile: Christian Democracy versus Marxist," British Journal of Sociology, Vol. XXI, No. 1 (March 1970), pp. 16-29.

16. On developments in administration and bureaucracy, see: Harry J. Benda, *The Pattern of Administrative Reforms in the Closing Years of Dutch Rule in Indonesia* (Reprint series, No. 16; New Haven, Conn.: Southeast Asia Studies, Yale University, 1965); Robert O. Tilman, *Bureaucratic Transition in Malaya* (Durham, N.C.: Duke University Press, 1964); Robert O. Tilman, "The bureaucratic legacy of modern Malaya," Indian Journal of Public Administration, Vol. IX, No. 2 (April-June 1963); Onofre D. Corpuz, *The Bureaucracy in the Philippines* (Quezon City: Institute of Public Administration, University of the Philippines, 1957); William J. Siffin, *The Thai Bureaucracy* (Honolulu: East West Center Press, 1966); Ralph Braibanti (ed.) *Asian Bureaucratic Systems Emergent from the British Imperial Tradition* (Durham, N.C.: Duke University Press, 1966); Hugh Tinker, "Structure of the British Imperial heritage," pp. 23-86; James Guyot, "Bureaucratic transformation in Burma," pp. 354-443; Bernard S. Cohn, "Recruitment and training of British civil servants in India," 1600-1860, pp. 87-140; David C. Potter, "Bureaucratic change in India," pp. 141-208; Ralph Braibanti, "The higher bureaucracy of Pakistan," pp. 209-353; Sir Charles Collins, "Ceylon: the imperial herigate," pp. 44-48; Robert N. Kearney, "Ceylon: the contemporary bureaucracy," pp. 485-549; Robert O. Tilman, "Bureaucratic development in Malaya," pp. 550-604; Merrill R. Goodall, "Administrative change in Nepal," pp. 605-642; and Ralph Braibanti, "Concluding observations," pp. 643-676. Abueva, loc. cit.; and Inayatullah, "Local administration in a developing country: the Pakistan case," in Weidner (ed.), op. cit., pp. 277-308.

17. On the development of the military in these countries, see: Moshe Lissak, "Center and periphery in developing countries and prototypes of military elites," Studies in Comparative International Development, Vol. V. No. 7 (1969-70).

In Latin America: Jose' Enrique Nums, "The new Latin American military coup," Studies in Comparative International Development, Vol. VI, No. 1 (1970-71); Jerry L. Weaver, "Political styles of the Guatemalan military elite," Studies in Comparative International Development, Vol. V, No. 4, (1969-70); and Julio Cotler, "Political crises and military populism in Peru," Studies in Comparative International Development, Vol. VI, No. 5 (1970-71).

In Southeast Asia: J. H. Badgley, "Burma's military government: a political analysis," Asian Survey, Vol. II, No. 6 (Aug. 1962), pp. 32-37; and William J. Pomeroy, *The*

Forest: A Personal Record of the Huk Guerilla Struggle in the Philippines (New York: International Publishers, 1963).

In the Middle East: Kenneth Fidel, "Military organization and conspiracy in Turkey," Studies in Comparative International Development, Vol. VI, No. 2 (1970-71).

18. On patterns of revolt and insurgency in these societies, see: Robert L. Solomon "Saya San and the Burmese rebellion," Modern Asian Studies, Vol. III, No. 3 (1969), pp. 209-233; Gabriel Gobron, *History and Philosophy of Caodaism* (Paris: Dervy 1949); George Coulet, *Les Sociétés Secrètes en Terre d'Annam* (Saigon: 1926); M. C. Guerrero, "The Colorum uprisings, 1924-1931," Asian Studies, Vol. V. (1967), pp. 65-78; Sartono Kartodiridjo, *The Peasants' Revolt of Banten in 1888. Its Conditions, Course and Sequel: A Case Study of Social Movements in Indonesia* (The Hague: M. Nijhoff, 1966); Harry J. Benda & Lance Castles, "The Samin movement," Bijdragen Tot de Tall-, Land-, en Volkenkunda, Vol. CXXV, No. 2 (1969), pp. 207-240; Harry J. Benda & Ruth McVey (eds.), *The Communist Uprisings of 1926-1927 in Indonesia: Key Documents* (Ithaca, N.Y.: Cornell University Press, 1960); B. Schrieke, *Indonesian Sociological Studies,* Part I, op. cit.; and James P. Harrison, *The Communists and Chinese Peasant Rebellions* (New York: Atheneum, 1969).

19. On educational problems and policies in some of these countries, see: J. W. G. Miller, *Education in Southeast Asia* (Sydney: Ian Novak, 1968), Ch. VIII, pp. 186-22(and Ch. X, pp. 255-284; Mudammed Shamul Hug, *Education and Development Strategy in South and Southeast Asia* (Honolulu: East West Center Press, 1965), pp. 17-21, 158-61 and 192-196; P. Foster, "The vocational school fallacy in development planning," in C. A. Anderson and M. J. Bowman (eds.), *Education and Economic Development* (Chicago: Aldine Publishing Company, 1965), pp. 142-166; C. A. Anderson, "Technical and vocational education in the new nations," in A. M. Kazamias and E. H. Epstein (eds.), *Schools in Transition: Essays in Comparative Education* (Boston: Allyn and Bacon, 1965), pp. 174-189; G. Ramanathan, *Educational Planning and National Integration* (London: Asia Publishing House, 1965); and Jorge Dominguez, *Education and Political and Social Development in Venezuela* (in preparation).

20. On agrarian reform and crises, see: Henry A. Landsberger (ed.), *Latin American Peasant Movements* (Ithaca, N.Y.: Cornell University Press, 1969); Anibal Quijano Obregon, "Tendencies in Peruvian development and class structure" in James Petras and Maurice Zeitlin (eds.), *Latin America: Reform or Revolution?* (Greenwich, Conn. Fawcett, 1968), pp. 289-328; Gerrit Huizer, "Peasant organization in the process of agrarian reform in Mexico," Studies in Comparative International Development, Vol. IV No. 6 (1968-69). Erich H. Jacoby, *Agrarian Unrest in Southeast Asia,* 2nd ed., rev & enl. (New York: Asia Publishing House, 1961); Doreen Warriner, *Land Reform in Principle and Practice* (Oxford: Clarendon Press, 1969); Ernest Feder, "Social opposition to peasant movements and its effect in Latin America," Studies in Comparative International Development, Vol. VI, No. 8 (1970-71); Frances L. Starner, *Magsaysay and the Philippine Peasantry: The Agrarian Impact on Philippine Politics, 1953-1956* (Berkeley, Calif.: University of California Press, 1961).

21. For more on this point see the literature cited in notes 14 and 15; and R.O. Tilman, *Man, State and Society in Contemporary Southeast Asia*, op. cit.

22. On regional problems, in addition to the literature on the political development of these states, see the general discussion in Geertz, *Old Societies and New States*, op. cit.

A good case study can be found in R. William Liddle, *Ethnicity, Party and National Integration: An Indonesian Case Study* (New Haven, Conn.: Yale University Press, 1!

23. On religion see, in addition to the literature above, Donald E. Smith, *South Asian Politics and Religion,* (Princeton University Press, 1966), *Religion and Politics in Burma* (Princeton, N.J.: Princeton University Press, 1965), *Religion and Political Development* (Boston: Little Brown, 1970).

24. On this point see Arend Lijphart, *The Politics of Accommodation: Pluralism and Democracy in the Netherlands* (Berkeley: University of California Press, 1968).

25. Specifically addressed to the problem of instability are: John L. Sorenson, "The social bases of instability in Southeast Asia," Asian Survey, Vol. IX, No. 7 (July 1969), pp. 540-545; Calvin A. Woodward, *The Growth of a Party System in Ceylon* (Providence, R. I.: Brown University Press, 1969); Soedjatmoko, "The rise of political parties in Indonesia," in Phillip W. Thayer (ed.), *Nationalism and Progress in Free Asia* (Baltimore, Md.: John Hopkins Press, 1956); J. H. Badgley, "Burma's political crisis," loc. cit.; John Wilson Lewis (ed.), *Party Leadership and Revolutionary Power in China* (Cambridge, Eng.: Cambridge University Press, 1970); Douglas A. Chalmers, "Crises and change in Latin America," Journal of International Affairs, Vol. XXIII, No. 1 (1969), pp. 76-78; and Leonard Schapiro, "Reflections on the changing role of the party in the totalitarian polity," Studies in Comparative Communism, Vol. II, No. 2, (April 1969).

On Ceylon, from this point of view, see: C. A. Woodward, *The Growth of a Party System in Ceylon* (Providence, R. I.: Brown University Press, 1969); James Jupp, "Constitutional developments in Ceylon since independence," Pacific Affairs, Vol. XLI (1968), pp. 169-183, and reply, Vol. XLIII (1970); and W. H. Wriggins, *Ceylon: Dilemmas of a New Nation* (Princeton, N. J.: Princeton University Press, 1960).

26. This follows the analysis in Eisenstadt, "Breakdowns of modernization," loc. cit.; see also Kemal Siddique, "Political development in Indonesia 1951-57: an evaluation of S. N. Eisenstadt's 'Breakdown of modernization'," (M. Soc. Sci. thesis, University of Singapore, 1970).

27. On the Maghreb, see: Samire Amin, *The Maghreb in the Modern World* (Hammondsworth, Penguin Books, 1970); Abdullah Laroui, *L'histoire du Maghreb* (Paris: Librairie Francois, Maspero, 1970); Yves Lacoste, *Ibn Khaldoun, Naissance de l'Histoire, Passe' du Tiersmonde* (Paris: François, Maspero, 1966); Charles F. Gallagher, *The United States and North Africa* (Cambridge, Mass.: Harvard University Press, 1963); C. Moore, *Politics of North Africa* (Boston: Little Brown, 1970); "Problematique du feodalisme hors d'Europe: le Maghreb précolonièle" in *Sur le Féodalisme* (Paris: Centre d'Etudes des Recherches Marxistes, Edition Sociales, 1971), pp. 145-247; and A. Vinogradov and John Waterbury, "Situations of contested legitimacy in Morocco: an alternative framework," Comparative Studies in Society and History, Vol. XIII, No. 1 (Jan. 1971), pp. 32-59.

28. On some of the problems of urbanization in these countries, see, for Latin America, John Friedmann, "The future of urbanization in Latin America," Studies in Comparative International Development, Vol. V, No. 9 (1969-70).

For Asia: P. M. Hauser (ed.), *Urbanisation in Asia and the Far East* (Paris: UNESCO, 1962; P. M. Hauser (ed.), *Urbanisation in the Far East* (Paris: UNESCO, 1960); and Hugh Tinker, "The city in the Asian polity," in Tinker, *Ballot Box and Bayonet* (London, New York: Oxford University Press, 1964).

For Southeast Asia: T. G. McGee, *The Southeast Asian City* (New York: Praeger, 1967); and Lance Castles, "The ethnic profile of Djakarta," Indonesia, Vol. III (April 1967), pp. 153-204.

29. See for details the bibliography above, especially in note 15.

30. For the range of political systems denoted as patrimonial see: S. N. Eisenstadt, "Patrimonial systems: introduction," in Eisenstadt (ed.), *Political Sociology,* op. cit., pp. 380-384; the discussion of the major characteristics of these societies is in part a summary and in part an extension of the discussion given there.

For materials on some of the most important cases of these historical societies, see the excerpts in: Eisenstadt (ed.), *Political Sociology,* op. cit., pp. 385 ff; William T. Sanders, "The central Mexican symbiotic region: a study in prehistoric settlement patterns," in Gordon R. Wilby (ed.) *Prehistoric Settlement Patterns in the New World* (New York: Viking Fund Publications in Anthropology, No. 23, 1956), pp. 115-127; Lawrence P. Briggs, "The ancient Khmer empire," Transactions of the American Philosophical Society, Vol. XLI, Part 1 (1951); Paul Pelliot, *Mémoire sur les coutumes du Cambodge de Tcheon Takouan* (Paris: Librairie d'Amerique et d'Orient, 1951); Sylvanus G. Morley, *The Ancient Maya,* 3rd ed. rev., by George W. Brainerd (Stanford, Calif.: Stanford University Press, 1956), Table VII, and p. 129; Michael D. Coe, "The funerary temple among the classic Maya," Southwestern Journal of Anthropoligy, Vol. XII, No. 4 (1956), pp. 387-394; George W. Brainerd, "Changing living patterns of the Yucatan Maya," American Antiquity, Vol. XXII, No. 2, Part I (1956), p. 162; William R. Bullard, "Maya settlement pattern in Northeastern Peten, Guatemala," American Antiquity, Vol. XXV, No. 3 (1960), pp. 355-372; E. H. C. Dobby, *Southeast Asia* (London: University of London Press, 1956); and George Groslier, *Recherches sur les Cambodgiens* (Paris: A. Challamel, 1921), pp. 21-23.

31. See, for instance: R. Heine-Geldern, "Conception of state and kinship in Southeast Asia," (Southeast Asian Program Data Paper, No. 18, Ithaca, N.Y., Cornell University, April 1956), pp. 1-13); Robert McCormick Adams, *The Evolution of Urban Society* (Chicago: Aldine, 1966); Paul Wheatley, *City as Symbol* (London: H. K. Lewis, 1969); and Paul Wheatley, *The Pivot of Four Quarters* (Edinburgh: Edinburgh University Press, 1971).

32. For analyses of selected cases of these societies, see in addition to the literature in note 1: F. W. Riggs, *Thailand: The Modernization of a Bureaucratic Polity* (Honolulu: East West Center Press, 1966); R. O. Winstedt, "Kinship and enthronement in Malaya," Journal of the Royal Asiatic Society, Malay Branch, Vol. XX, Part 1 (June 1947), pp. 129-139; Thaung, "Burmese kingship in theory and practice under the reign of King Mindon," Journal of the Burma Research Society. Vol. XLII, No. 2 (1959), pp. 17185; Ma Kyan, "King Mindon's Councillors," Journal of the Burma Research Society, Vol. XLIV, No. 1 (1961), pp. 43-60; Yi Yi, "The judicial system of King Mindon," Journal of the Burma Research Society. Vol. XLIV, No. 2 (1961), pp. 7-28; J. D. Legge, *Indonesia* (Englewood Cliffs, N. J.: Prentice Hall, 1964.); B. Schrieke, *Indonesian Sociological Studies* (The Hague, Bandung: Van Hoeve, 1955), Part I.: "The causes and effects of communism on the West coast of Sumatra"; B. Schrieke, *Indonesian Sociological Studies* (The Hague, Bandung: W. Van Hoeve, 1957), Part II, "Ruler and realm in early Java"; J. C. Van Lear, *Indonesian Trade and Society* (The Hague, Bandung: W. Van Hoeve, 1955), pp. 1-221; O. W. Wolters, *Early Indonesian Commerce* (Ithaca, N.Y.: Cornell University Press, 1967); Prapanca, Rakawi of Majaphit, *Java in the Fourteenth Century: A Study in Cultural History,* Ed. and trans. Theodore Pigeaud (5 Vols., The Hague: M. Nijhoff, 1960-63); Soemarsaid Moertono, *State and Statecraft in Old Java: A Study of the Later Mataram Period, Sixteenth to Nineteenth Century* (Ithaca, N.Y.: Modern Indonesia Project, Southeast Asia Program, Dept. of Asian Studies, Cornell University, 1968); Jean Moura (Simone Louvet), *Le Royaume de Cambodge* (2 Vols. Paris: E. Leroux,

1883); Solange Theirry, "La personne sacrée du roi dans la littérature populaire Cambodgienne," Studies in the History of Religions, Vol. IV (1959); Charles Meyer, "Les mystérieuses relations entre la roi du Cambodge et les 'Patao' des Jarai," Etudes Cambodgiennes, Vol. IV. (Oct.-Dec. 1965), pp. 14-26; Kamil Krofta, "Bohemia to the extention of the Premyslids," Cambridge Medieval History (Cambridge, Eng.: Cambridge University Press, 1936), Vol. VI, pp. 422-447, and "Bohemia in the fourteenth century," ibid., Vol. VII, pp. 155-182; Bertold Spuler, *The Muslim World*, trans. F. R. C. Bagdy (Leiden: E. J. Brill, 1960); John Adams and Nancy Hancock, "Land and economy in traditional Vietnam," Journal of Southeast Asian Studies, Vol I, No. 2 (Sept. 1970) pp. 90-98; Bernard Fall, "The political religious sects of Vietnam," Pacific Affairs, Vol. XXVIII, No. 3 (Sept. 1955), pp. 235-253; and John K, Whitmore, *Vietnamese Adaptations of Chinese Government Structure in the Fifteenth Century* (New Haven, Conn.: Yale University, Southeast Asian Studies, 1970).

33. For greater detail, see: Max Weber, "Representation" in Eisenstadt (ed.), *Political Sociology*. op. cit., pp. 308-384; S. N. Eisenstadt, "Patrimonial systems: introduction" in ibid., and Delany, op. cit.

34. On these types of polities, see S. N. Eisenstadt, *The Political Systems of Empires* (New York: Free Press, 1963), especially Ch. 7.

35. B. F. Hoselitz, *Sociological Aspects of Economic Growth* (New York: Free Press, 1960), pp. 85-114.

36. G. Dalton, *Primitive Archaic and Modern Economics: Essays of Karl Polanyi* (New York: Anchor Books, 1968), especially Ch. i: "Societies and economic system," pp. 3-20; Ch. ix: "Redistribution," pp. 207-238; and Ch. ixxx: "Posts of trade in early societies," pp. 238-261; and K. Polanyi, C. M. Arensberg and Harry W. Pearson, *Trade and Market in Early Empires* (Glencoe: The Free Press, 1957).

37. For a general analysis, see S. N. Eisenstadt, "Patrimonial systems: introduction," loc. cit.

For more detailed description of nomadic patrimonial systems, see, for instance, L. Krader, "Principles and structures in the organization of the Asiatic steppe-pastorialists," in Eisenstadt (ed.) *Political Sociology*, op. cit., pp. 146-156, and the works cited in note 33, above.

38. See, for instance G. Vernadskii, "The scope and contents of Genghis Khan's Yasa," Harvard Journal of Asiatic Studies, Vol. III (1938), pp. 337-380; and Spuler, op. cit.

39. On these concepts, see S. N. Eisenstadt, "Bureaucracy, bureaucratization, markets and power structure" in Eisenstadt (ed.), *Essays in Comparative Institutions* (New York: Wiley & Sons, 1965), especially pp. 175-195.

40. For detailed descriptions, see the works cited in notes 33 and 38 above, and also, E. R. Leach, "The frontiers of Burma," Comparative Studies in Society and History, Vol. III, No. 1 (Oct. 1960), pp. 49-68.

41. See, Abdullah Laroui, *L'histoire du Maghreb* (Paris: Librairie François Maspero, 1970); and in more general terms: Michael D. Coe, "Social typology and the tropical forest civilization," Comparative Studies in Society and History, Vol. IV, No. 1 (1961), pp. 65-83.

42. On Middle Eastern tribal federations, see the readings in S. N. Eisenstadt (ed.), *Political Sociology*, op. cit.; and Adams, op. cit.

43. On ancient Egypt, see H. Kees, "Agyten" in Handbuch der Altertumseissenschaft (Munich: C. H. Beck, 1933), Vol. III, No. 1.

On Ceylon: R. Pieris, *Sinhalese Social Organization: The Kendya Period* (Colombo: Ceylon University Press, Board, 1956).

44. On Iran, see: Arthur E. Christensen, *L'Itan sous les Sassanides,* 2nd ed. (Copenhagen: E. Munksgaard, 1944); and M. Ehtecham (M. Ihtisham), *L'Itan sous les Achemenides* (Dissertation, Lausanne, Fribourg, Switzerland, 1946).

45. This largely follows the analysis presented in S. N. Eisenstadt (ed.) *Political Sociology,* op. cit., and *The Political Systems of Empires,* op. cit.

46. On this piont see: E. Swanson, *Rules of Descent,* "Studies in the sociology of parentage" (Ann Arbor, Mich: Anthropological Papers, Museum of Anthropology, University of Michigan, 1969); George Peter Murdock (ed.), *Social Structure in Southeast Asia* (Chicago: Quadrangle Books, 1960); and R. T. Holt, "Comparative political and comparative administration," in Fred W. Riggs (ed.), *Frontiers of Development Administration* (Durham, N. C.: Duke University Press, 1970), pp. 305-325.

47. On Japan see: R. N. Bellah, "Values and social change in modern Japan," Asian Cultural Studies, No. 3 (Mitaka, Tokyo: International Christian University, Oct. 1962); Edwin O. Reischauer and John K. Fairbank, *East Asia, The Great Tradition* (Boston: Houghton Mifflin & Co., 1958); R. N. Bellah, *Tokugawa Religion* (Glencoe: The Free Press, 1957); R. N. Bellah, "Continuity and change in Japanese society," in Bernard Barber & Alex Inkeles (eds.), *Stability and Social Change* (Boston: Little Brown, 1971), pp. 377-407; M. B. Jansen (ed.), *Changing Japanese Attitudes Toward Modernization* (Princeton, N.J.: Princeton University Press, 1965); Herbert Passin, "Japanese society," *International Encyclopedia of the Social Sciences,* Vol. VIII, pp. 236-249; and R. N. Bellah, "Japan's cultural identity," Journal of Asian Studies, Vol. XXIV, No. 24 (Aug. 1965), pp. 573-594.

On China see: Etienne Balazs, *Chinese Civilization and Bureaucracy: Variations on a Theme* (New Haven, Conn: Yale University Press, 1964); and S. N. Eisenstadt, *The Political Systems of Empires,* op. cit., pp. 323-333

On Vietnam see Alexander Woodside, *Vietnam and the Chinese Model* (Cambridge, Mass.: Harvard University Press, 1970).

48. This analysis follows the introduction to "Patrimonial systems" in Eisenstadt (ed.), *Political Sociology,* op. cit., Chapter V.

49. On the system of stratification of these societies see especially Hans-Dieter Evers (ed.), *Loosely Structured Social Systems: Thailand in Comparative Perspective* ("Cultural Report Series," No. 17, New Haven Conn.: Yale University Southeast Asia Studies, 1969).

See also L. H. Palmier, *Social Status and Power in Java* ("Monographs on social anthropoligy," London: London School of Economics, 1960, 1969).

For the technical use of the term 'prestige' as will be employed here and in subsequent analyses see S. N. Eisenstadt, "Prestige, participation and strata formation" in J. A. Jackson (ed.) *Sociological Studies,* Vol. I (Cambridge, Eng.: Cambridge University Press, 1968), pp. 62-103 and S. N. Eisenstadt, *Social Differentiation and Stratification* (Glencoe, Ill.: Scott & Foresman, 1971), esp. Chs. 1-5.

50. See for instance M. A. P. Meilink-Roelofsz, *Asian Trade & European Influence in the Indonesian Archipelago between 1500 and about 1630* (The Hague: M. Nijhoff, 1962).

51. On such movements see: Harry J. Benda, "Peasant movements in colonial Southeast Asia," Asian Studies, Vol. III, No. 3 (Dec. 1965), pp. 420-434; Harry J.

Benda, "The structure of Southeast Asian history: some preliminary observations," The Journal of Southeast Asian History, Vol. III, No. 1 (March, 1962); Frances Hills, "Millenarian machines in South Vietnam," Comparative Studies in Society & History, Vol. XIII, No. 3 (July 1971), pp. 325-350; and Bernard Dahm, "Leadership and mass response in Java, Burma and Vietnam," Paper presented to the International Congress of Orientalists, Canberra, 1971 (Photocopied, Kiel University).

On various movements of revolt, see also: Milton Osborne, *Region of Revolt: Focus on Southeast Asia* (Sydney: Pergamon Press, 1970); and J. Van der Kroef, "Javanese messianic expectations: their origin and cultural context," Comparative Studies in Society and History, Vol. I (1959), pp. 299-323.

52. On these conceptions of the social and religious order, see, in addition to the materials on general history and political development of these countries: Sami A. Hahha and George H. Gardner (eds.) *Arab Socialism* (Leiden: E. J. Brill, 1969); A. J. D. Matz, "The dynamics of change in Latin America," Journal of Inter American Studies, Vol. XI, No. 1 (Jan. 1966), pp. 66-76; Donald E. Worcester, "The Spanish-American past, enemy of change," Journal of Inter-American Studies, Vol. XI, No. 1 (Jan. 1969), pp. 66; Klaman Silvert, "Latin America and its alternative future," International Journal, Vol. XXIV, No. 3 (Summer 1969), pp. 403-44; Merida Blanco, "Ideology and social change: the Mexican revolution," Social Relations (Feb. 1966); Hans-Dieter Evers, *Kulturwandel in Ceylon* (Baden-Baden: Berlag Lutzeyer, August 1964; Emanuel Sarkisyanz, *Buddhist Backgrounds of the Burmese Revolution* (The Hague: M. Nijhoff, 1965); Donald E. Smith, *Religion and Politics in Burma*, op. cit.; Mi Mi Khaing, *Burmese Family* (Bombay: Longmans, Green, 1947); Charles F. Gallagher, "Contemporary Islam: a frontier of communalism. Aspects of Islam in Malaysia," American Universities Field Staff Reports, Southeast Asia Series, Vol. XIV, No. 10 (1966); James Peacock, *Rites of Modernization: Symbols and Social Aspects of Indonesian Proletarian Drama* (Chicago: University of Chicago Press, 1968); and R. N. Milton, "The basic Malay house," Journal of the Royal Asiatic Society, Malay Branch, Vol. XXIX, No. 3 (1965), pp. 145-155.

53. See the works cited in note 15, as well as: Jan M. Pluvier, *Confrontations: A Study in Indonesian Politics* (Kuala Lumpur: Oxford University Press, 1965); Herbert Feith and Lance Castles (eds.), *Indonesian Political Thinking, 1945-1965* (Ithaca, N. Y.: Cornell University Press, 1970); and Benedict Anderson, "The language of Indonesian politics," Indonesia, No. I (April 1966), pp. 89-116.

54. On the patterns of Stratification in these societies, see: Magali Sarfatti and A. E. Berman, *Social Stratification in Peru* ("Politics and Modernization Series," No. 5, Berkeley: Institute of International Studies, University of California, 1969), pp. 43, 52-54; B. G. Burnett and R. F. Johnson (eds.), *Political Forces in Latin America* (Belmont, Calif.: Wadsworth Publishing Co., 1968), esp. R. L. Peterson, "Guatemala, Honduras, El Salvador and Nicaragua," p. 76, J. B. Gabbert, "Ecuador," pp. 284-287) and B. G. Burnett, "Chile", pp. 384-394; Jorge Graciarena, *Poder y Sociales en el Desarollo de América Latina* (Buenos Aires: Paidos, 1968); Gino Germani, *Politica y Sociedad in una Epoca de Transicion*, 2nd ed. (Buenos Aires: Paidos, 1968); D. B. Heath and R. N. Adams (eds.), *Contemporary Cultures and Societies in Latin America* (New York: Random House, 1965), esp. Part III, "Social Organization"; J. Peacock, *Rites of Modernization*, op. cit.; F. Bourricaud, "Structure and function of the Peruvian oligarchy," Studies in Comparative International Development, Vol. I (1965), Vol. II (1966); Alaine Touraine, "Social mobility, class relations, and nationalism in Latin America," Studies in Comparative International Development, Vol. I (1965); S. M. Lipset and A. Solari (eds.) *Elites in Latin America*

(New York: Oxford University Press, 1967), esp. F. Bonilla, "Cultural elites," pp. 242-249; J. Lopez, "Etude de quelque changements fondamentauz dans la politique et la societe Bresiliennes," Sociologie du Travail, No. VII (1965), pp. 238-253; M. G. Navarro, "Mexico: the lop-sided revolution," in Claudio Veliz (ed.) Obstacles to Change in Latin America (London, New York: Oxford University Press), p. 222; P. Gonzalez-Casanova, "L'evolution du système des classes au Mexique," Cahiers Internationaux de Sociologie, Vol. XXXIX (1965); Manning Nash, The Golden Road to Modernity (New York: Wiley & Sons, 1965); B. Ryan, Caste in Modern Ceylon (New Brunswick, N. J.: Rutgers University Press, 1953); B. Ryan, "The Ceylonese villages and the new value system," Rural Sociology, Vol. XVII, No. 4 (1952), pp. 311-321; Fernando H. Cardoso, "Le proletariat Brésilien: situation et comportment social," Sociologie du Travail, Vol. III, No. 4 (1961), pp. 50-65; O. Sunkel, "Change and frustration in Chile" in Veliz (ed.), op. cit., pp. 129, 131; G. A. Dillon Soaves, "The politics of universal development: the case of Brazil" in S. M. Lipset and S. Rokkan (eds.), Party System and Voter Alignments: Cross National Perspective (New York: Free Press, 1967), pp. 467-498; and Alain Touraine and Daniel Pecaut, "Working class consciousness and economic development," Studies in Comparative International Development, Vol. III, No. 4 (1967-68).

A general discussion of these patterns of stratification is given in S. N. Eisenstadt, Social Differentiation and Stratification (Glencoe, Ill.: Scott Foresman, 1971).

55. See the discussion on this in S. N. Eisenstadt, Social Differentiation and Stratification, op. cit., esp. Chs. IX-XII.

56. Very good materials on this problem are collected in R. O. Tilman, Man, State and Society in Contemporary Southeast Asia, op. cit., and the literature cited in note 15.

57. On the colonial setting, see: J. S. Furnivall, Colonial Policy and Practice, op. cit; V. Turner (ed.), Colonisation in Africa, op. cit.; S. N. Eisenstadt, Essays on Social and Political Aspects of Economic Development, op. cit.; E. Wallerstein, op. cit.; and Harry J. Benda, "Political elites in colonial Southeast Asia: an historical analysis," Comparative Studies in Society and History, Vol. VII, No. 3 (April 1965).

58. For one of the best expositions of the problem of dependence, see Celso Furtado, Obstacles to Development in Latin America (New York: Anchor Books, 1970).

See also the literature on the economic problems of these countries cited in note 14, as well as Howard F. Cline (ed.), Latin American History, Vol. II (Austin, Texas: University of Texas Press, 1967), esp. Miron Burgin, "Research in Latin American economics and economic history," pp. 466-475; Charles C. Griffin, "Economic and social aspects of the era of Spanish-American independence," pp. 485-494; and Sanford A. Mosk, "Latin American economics: the field and its problems," pp. 495-499.

59. On rebellion and revolts in these societies, see note 18 and also: Milton Osborne, op. cit.; Harry J. Benda, "Peasant movements in colonial Southeast Asia," loc. cit; G. Rairbairn, Revolutionary Warfare and Communist Strategy (London: Faber, 1968); David Galula, Counterinsurgency Warfare (New York: Praeger, 1964); E. H. Jacoby, op. cit.; George K. Taham, Communist Revolutionary Warfare, 2nd ed. (New York: Praeger, 1967); and Frank N. Trager (ed.), Marxism in Southeast Asia (Stanford, Calif.: Stanford University Press, 1959).

60. One instance of such development is analyzed in M. Ames, "Ideological and social change in Ceylon," Human Organization, Vol. XXII, No. 1 (1963), pp. 45-53.

61. See R. Kothari, *Politics in India* (Boston: Little Brown, 1969).

62. See David Easton, *A System Analysis of Political Life* (New York: Wiley & Sons, 1965), Chs. 11-13.

63. For an analysis of the different crises and their outcomes in some of these countries, in addition to the literature quoted above, it may be useful to peruse the reports published by the American University Field Staff (A.U.F.S.), including especially the following: Willard A. Hanna, "The Indonesia crisis: mid-1964 phase," A.U.F.S., Vol. III, No. 7; Willard A. Hanna, "Re-reviving a revolution," A.U.F.S., Vol. XI, No. 4; Willard A. Hanna, "The Indonesia crisis: early 1963 phase," A.U.F.S., Vol. XI, No. 8; Albert Ravenholt, "A note on the Philippines," A.U.F.S., Vol. X, No. 8; Willard A. Hanna, "Modes of modernization in Southeast Asia," A.U.F.S., Vol. XVII, No. 3; Louis Dupree, "A note on Pakistan," A.U.F.S., Vol. VII, No. 8; Louis Dupree, "Pakistan: 1964-1966. Part I: the government and the opposition," A.U.F.S., Vol. X., No. 5; Louis Dupree, "Pakistan: 1964-1965. Part III: the economy and the five year plans," A.U.F.S., Vol. X, No. 7; Alan W. Horton, "Syrian stability and the Baath," A.U.F.S., Vol. XIV, No. 1; John Hanessian, Jr., "Iranian land reform," A.U.F.S., Vol. XII, No. 10; Richard W. Patch, "The last of Bolivia's MnR?," A.U.F.S., Vol. XI, No. 5; Richard W. Patch, "Bolivia's nationalism and the military," A.U.F.S., Vol. XVI, No. 3; Richard W. Patch, "The Peruvian agrarian reform bill," A.U.F.S., Vol. XI, No. 3; Richard W. Patch, "A note on Bolivia and Peru," A.U.F.S., Vol. IX, No. 4; Richard W. Patch, "Peru's new president and agrarian reform," A.U.F.S., Vol. X, No. 2; Richard W. Patch, "A note on Bolivia and Peru," A.U.F.S., Vol. XII, No. 2; K. H. Silvert, "A note on Chile and Argentina," A.U.F.S., Vol. VIII, No. 8; James G. Maddox, "Mexican land reform," A.U.F.S., JGH 5 57 NY57.James W. Rowe, "Argentina's restless military," A.U.F.S., Vol. XI, No. 2; James W. Row, "Argentina: an election retrospect," A.U.F.S., Vol. XI, No. 1; K. H. Silvert, "Nationalism and the role of elites in Latin America," A.U.F.S., Vol. I, No. 2, 1959; James W. Rowe, "Revolution or counterrevolution in Brasil? Part II: From 'Black Friday' to the New Reforms," A.U.F.S., Vol. XI, No. 5; James W. Rowe, "The 'revolution' and the 'system': notes on Brazilian politics. Part I: Seeds of the system," A.U.F.S., Vol. XII, No. 3; James W. Rowe, "The 'revolution' and the 'system': notes on Brazilian politics. Part II: The 'system'–full flower and crisis," A.U.F.S., Vol. XII, No. 4; and James W. Rose, "The 'revolution' and the 'system': notes on Brazilian politics. Part III: The 'revolution'–generals and technocrats," A.U.F.S., Vol. XII, No. 5.

64. An interesting analysis of contemporary Egypt from this point of view can be found in Ronald Segal, "The new Egypt," Jerusalem Post, May 7, 1971. And of special interest is also Philippe C. Schmitter, *Interest, Conflict and Political Change in Brazil* (Stanford, California: Stanford University Press, 1971); and David Lehmann, "Political incorporation versus political stability: the case of the Chilean agrarian reform, 1965-70," Journal of Development Studies, Vol. I, No. 4 (July 1971).

65. On extremist movements, see the literature cited in note 18 and also: K. Silvert, *The Conflict Society, Reaction and Revolution in Latin America* (New Orleans: Hauser Press, 1962); David Chaplin, "Peru's postponed revolution," World Politics, Vol. XX, No. 3 (April 1968), pp. 393-420; Robert N. Burr (ed.), "Latin America's nationalistic revolution," Annals of the American Academy of Political and Social Science, (March 1961); Touraine and Pecaut, op. cit.; C.A.M. Hennessy, "Shifting forces in the Bolivian revolution," The World Today, Vol. XX, No. 5 (1964), pp. 197-208; R. J. Alexander, *The Bolivian National Revolution* New Brunswick, N.J.: Rutgers Univesity Press, 1958); Jacques Decornoy, "Ceylon, naissance

d'une révolution," le Monde (June 16, 17 and 18, 1971); James Petras, "Revolution and guerilla movements in Latin America: Venezuela, Guatemala, Colombia, and Peru," in Petras and Zeitlin (eds.) op. cit., pp. 329-369; Eduardo Galeano, "With the guerillas in Guatemala" in ibid, pp. 370-380; and Touraine and Pecaut, op. cit.

66. This analysis is an extension of the argument in S. N. Eisenstadt, *Social Differentiation and Stratification* (Glenview, Ill.: Scott Foresman & Co., 1971).

67. See on this point the detailed analysis in D. Katz and R. L. Kahn, *The Social Psychology of Organization* New York: John Wiley & Sons Inc., 1966), pp. 14-22.

68. See S. N. Eisenstadt, "Prestige, participation and strata-formation," in J.A. Jackson (ed.), Sociological Studies, Vol. I, Cambridge College Press, 1968, pp. 62-103.

69. See S. N. Eisenstadt "Some observations on the dynamics of traditions," in *Comparative Studies in Society and History*, Vol. 11, No. 4 (October 1969), pp. 451-475.

70. See S. N. Eisenstadt, *Intellectuals and Traditions*, in Daedalus, Spring, 1972 and Robert F. Murphy, *The Dialection of Social Life* (New York: Basic Books, 1971).

71. Some such possibilities are discussed in S. N. Eisenstadt, *The Protestant Ethic and Modernization* (New York: Basic Books, 1968), ix-407 pp.

72. See on this point S.N. Eisenstadt, "Social institutions: comparative study," *International Encyclopaedia of Social Sciences* (New York: Macmillan Co., 1968), pp. 421-429.

73. This follows S. N. Eisenstadt, "Social change, differentiation and evolution," American Sociological Review, Vol. 29, No. 3 (June 1964), pp. 375-386.

Bibliography

ADAMS, J., N. HANCOCK (1970) "Land and economy in traditional Vietnam," Journal of Southeast Asian Studies, Vol. 1, No. 2 (September).

ADAMS, R. M. (1966) The Evolution of Urban Society. Chicago: Aldine.

AKIN RABIBHADANA (1969) The Organization of Thai Society in the Early Bangkok Period, 1782-1873. Ithaca: Cornell University Press.

ALEXANDER, R. J. The Bolivian National Revolution. New Brunswick: Rutgers University Press.

AMES, M. (1963) "Ideological and social change in Ceylon," Human Organization, Vol. 22, No. 1.

ANDERSON, B. (1966) "The language of Indonesian politics," Indonesia, No. 1 (April).

ANDERSON, C. A. (1965) "Technical and vocational education in the new nations," in A. M. Kazamias and E. H. Epstein (eds.) Schools in Transition: Essays in Comparative Education. Boston: Allyn & Bacon.

AZMORA, M. D. (1967) (ed.) Studies in Philippine Anthropoligy in Honor of H. Otley Beyer. Quezon City: Alemar-Phoenix.

BADGLEY, J. H. (1963) "Burma, the nexus of socialism and two political traditions," Asian Survey, Vol. 6, No. 2: 89-96 (February).

––– (1962) "Burma's military government: a political analysis," Asian Survey, Vol. 2, No. 6 (August).

––– (1958) "Burma's political crisis," Pacific Affairs, Vol. 30, No. 4: 336-352 (December).

––– (1956) "Burma's political crisis" in P. W. Thayer (ed.). Nationalism and Progre in Free Asia. Baltimore: Johns Hopkins Press.

BALAZS, E. (1964) Chinese Civilization and Bureaucracy: Variations on a Theme. New Haven: Yale University Press.

BASTIN, J. (1967) (ed.) The Emergence of Modern Southeast Asia: 1511-1957. Englewood Cliffs: Prentice Hall.

BASTIN, J. and H. J. BENDA (1968) A History of Modern Southeast Asia. Englewood Cliffs: Prentice Hall.

BELLAH, R. N. (1971) "Continuity and change in Japanese society," in B. Barber and A. Inkeles, eds. Stability and Social Change, Boston: Little Brown

––– (1965) (ed.) Religion and Progress in Modern Asia. New York: Free Press.

BENDA, H. J. (1965) The Pattern of Administrative Reforms in the Closing Years of Dutch Rule in Indonesia. New Haven: Southeast Asia Studies, Reprint series No. 16, Yale University.

––– (1965) "Peasant movements in colonial Southeast Asia," Asian Studies, Vol. 3, No. 3 (December).

––– (1962) "The structure of Southeast Asian history: some preliminary observations," Journal of Southeast Asian History, Vol. 3, No. 1 (March).

––– "Political elites in colonial Southeast Asia: an historical analysis," Comparative Studies in Society and History, Vol. 7, No. 3 (April).

–––, L. CASTLES (1969) "The Samin movement," Bijdragen Tot de Tall-, Land-, en Volkenkunda, Vol. 125, No. 2.

–––, R. McVEY (1960) The Communist Uprisings of 1926-1927 in Indonesia: Key Documents. Ithaca: Cornell University Press.

BENDIX, R. (1967) "Tradition and modernity reconsidered," Comparative Studies in Society and History, Vol. 9, No. 3: 292-293 (April).

BLACK, C. E. (1966) The Dynamics of Modernization. New York: Harper & Row.

BLANCO, M. (1966) "Ideology and social change: the Mexican revolution," Social Relations (February).

BOURRICAUD, F. (1965-1966) "Structure and function of the Peruvian oligarchy," Studies in Comparative International Development, Vols. 1 and 2.

BRAIBANTI, R. (1966) (ed.) Asian Bureaucratic Systems Emergent from the British Imperial Tradition. Durham: Duke University Press.

BRAINERD, G. W. (1956) "Changing living patterns of the Yucatan Maya," American Antiquity, Vol. 22, No. 2, Part 1.

BRIGGS, L. P. (1951) "The ancient Khmer empire," Transactions of the American Philosophical Society, Vol. 41, Part 1.

BULLARD, W. R. (1960) "Maya settlement patterns in northeastern Petern, Guatemala," American Antiquity, Vol. 25, No. 3.

BURNETT, B. G., R. R. JOHNSON (1968) (eds.) Political Forces in Latin America. Belmont: Wadsworth.

BURR, R. N. (1961) (ed.) "Latin America's Nationalistic Revolution'" Annals of the American Academy of Political and Social Science (March).

CADY, J. F. (1960) A History of Modern Burma. Ithaca: Cornell University Press.

CARDOSO, F. H. (1961) "Le proletariat Brésilien: situation et comportment social," Sociologie du Travail, Vol. 3, No. 4.

CARLETON, A. (1950) "The Syrian coups d'etat of 1949," Middle East Journal, Vol. 4.

CASTLES, L. (1967) "The ethnic profile of Djakarta," Indonesia, Vol. 3 (April). Centre d'Etudes des Recherches Marxistes (1971) "Problematique du féodalisme hors d'Europe: le Mahgreb précoloniele," in Sur le féodalisme. Paris: Edition Sociales.

CHALMERS, D. A. (1969) "Crises and change in Latin America," Journal of International Affairs, Vol. 23, No. 1.

CHAPLIN, D. (1968) "Peru's postponed revolution," World Politics, Vol. 20, No. 3 (April).

CHRISTENSEN, A. E. (1944) L'Itan sous les Sassanides. Copenhagen: Manksgaard.

CLINE, H. F. (1967) Latin American History, Vol. 2. Austin: University of Texas Press.

COE, M. D. (1961) "Social typology and the tropical forest civilization," Comparative Studies in Society and History, Vol. 4, No. 1.

———(1956) "The funerary temple among the classic Maya," Southwestern Journal of Anthropology, Vol. 12, No. 4.

CORPUZ, O. D. (1957) The Bureaucracy in the Philippines. Quezon City: Institute of Public Administration, University of the Philippines.

COTLER, J. (1970-1971) "Political crises and military populism in Peru," Studies in Comparative International Development, Vol. 6, No. 5.

COULET, G. (1926) Les Sociétés en Terre d'Annam. Saigon.

DAHM, B. (n.d.) "Leadership and mass response in Java, Burma and Vietnam." Paper sented to the International Congress of Orientalists, Canberra, (Photocopied, Kiel University).

DALTON, G. (1968) Primitive, Archaic and Modern Economics: Essays of Karl Polanyi. New York: Anchor Books.

DECORNOY, J. (1971) "Ceylon, naissance d'une révolution," le Monde, June 16, 17, 18.

DELANY, W. (1963) "The development and decline of patrimonial and bureaucratic administrations," Administrative Science Quarterly, Vol. 17, No. 4: 458-501 (March).

DILLON SOAVES, G. A. (1967) "The politics of universal development: the case of Brazil," in S. M. Lipset and S. Rokkan (eds.) Party System and Voter Alignments: Cross National Perspective. New York: Free Press.

DOBBY, E. H. C. (1956) Southeast Asia. London: University of London Press.

DOMINQUEZ, J. Education and Political and Social Development in Venezuela. (In preparation).

DUMONT, J. J. (1966) "Le Conflit 'sociétal' et le processus de changment politique et économique. Le case de la 'violenua' et Colombie," Civilizatione, Vol. 16, No. 2

DUNCANSON, D. J. (1969) "Vietnam as a nation-state," Modern Asian Studies, Vol. 3. No. 2.

DUPREE, L. "Pakistan: 1964-1965. Part 3: the economy and the five-year plans," A.U.F.S., Vol. 10, No. 7

——— "Pakistan: 1964-1966. Part 1: the government and the opposition," A.U.F.S., Vol. 10, No. 5.

——— "A note on Pakistan," A.U.F.S., Vol. 7, No. 8.

FASTON, D. (1965) A System Analysis of Political Life (Chapters 11-13). New York: Wiley.

EGGAN, F., E. HESTER and N. GINSBURG (1965) (eds.) Area Handbook on the Philippines. Chicago: University of Chicago for H.R.A.F.

EHTECHAM, M. (1946) L'Itan Sous l'Achemenides. Dissertation, Lausanne, Fribourg Switzerland.

EISENSTADT, S. N. (1971) "Intellectuals and traditions," Daedalus (Spring).

——— (1971) "General introduction: the scope and problems of political sociology," in Eisenstadt (ed.) Political Sociology. New York: Basic Books.

––– (1971) "Patrimonial systems: introduction" in Eisenstadt (ed.) Political Sociology.

––– (1971) Social Differentiation and Stratification. Glencoe: Scott, Foresman.

––– (1969) "Some observations on the dynamics of traditions," Comparative Studies in Society and History, Vol. 2, No. 4 (October).

––– (1968) "Prestige, participation and strata-formation," in J. A. Jackson (ed.) Sociological Studies, Vol. 1, Cambridge College Press.

––– (1968) The Protestant Ethic and Modernization. New York: Basic Books.

––– (1968) "Reflections on a theory of modernization," in A. Rivkin (ed.) Nations by Design: Institution Building in Africa. Garden City, N.Y.: Anchor Books.

––– (1968) "Social institutions: comparative study," International Encyclopeadia of the Social Sciences. New York: Macmillan.

––– (1968) "Some new looks at the problem of relations between traditional societies and modernization," Economic Development and Cultural Change, Vol. 16, No. 3 (April).

––– (1965) "Bureaucracy, bureaucratization, markets and power structure," in Eisenstadt (ed.) Essays in Comparative Institutions. New York: Wiley.

––– (1964) "Breakdowns of modernization," Economic Development and Cultural Change," Vol. 12, No. 4 (July).

––– (1964) "Social change, differentiation and evolution," American Societal Review, Vol. 29, No. 3 (June).

––– (1963) The Political Systems of Empires. New York: Free Press.

––– (1958) Essays on Social and Political Aspects of Economic Development. The Hague: Mouton.

EMERSON, R. (1960) From Empire to Nation: The Rise to Self-Assertion of Asian and African Peoples. Cambridge: Harvard University Press.

EVERS, H-D. (1969) Loosely Structured Social Systems: Thailand in Comparative Perspective. Cultural Report Series, No. 17. New Haven: Southeast Asia Studies, Yale University.

––– (1964) Kulturwandel in Ceylon. Baden-Baden: Berlag Lutzeyer.

FALL, B. (1955) "The political religious sects of Vietnam," Pacific Affairs, Vol. 28, No. 3 (September).

FEDER, E. (1970-1971) "Social opposition to peasant movements and its effect in Latin America," Studies in Comparative International Development, Vol. 6, No. 8.

FEITH, H., L. CASTLES, (1970) (eds.) Indonesian Political Thinking, 1945-1965. Ithaca: Cornell University Press.

FIDEL, K. (1970-1971) "Military organization and conspiracy in Turkey," Studies in Comparative International Development, Vol. 6, No. 2.

FITZGIBBON, R. H. (1960) "Dictatorship and democracy in Latin America," International Affairs, Vol. 36, No. 1 (January).

FOSTER, P. (1965) "The vocational school fallacy in development planning," in C. A. Anderson and M. J. Bowman (eds.) Education and Economic Development. Chicago: Aldine.

FRIEDMAN, H. J. (1961) "Notes on Pakistan's basic democracies," Asian Survey, Vol. 1, No. 10 (December).

––– (1960) "Pakistan's experiment in basic democracies," Pacific Affairs, Vol. 33, No. 2 (June).

FRIEDMANN, J. (1969-1970) "The future of urbanization in Latin America," Studies in Comparative International Development, Vol. 5, No. 9.

FURNIVAL, J. S. (1960) The Governance of Modern Burma. New York: Institute of Pacific Relations.

––– (1948), 1956) Colonial Policy and Practice: A Comparative Study of Burma and Netherlands India. Cambridge: Cambridge University Press. New York: New York University Press.

FURTADO, C. (1970) Obstacles to Development in Latin America. New York: Anchor.

GALEANO, E. "With the guerillas in Guatemala" ibid.

GALLAGHER, C. F. (1966) "Contemporary Islam: a frontier of communalism. Aspects of Islam in Malaysia," American Universities Field Staff Reports, South East Asia Series, Vol. 14. No. 10.

GALLAGHER, C. F. (1963) The United States and North Africa. Cambridge: Harvard University Press.

GALULA, D. (1964) Counterinsurgency Warfare, New York: Praeger.

GEERTZ, C. (1963) "Primordial sentiments and civil policies in the new states," in Geertz (ed.) Old Societies and New States. Chicago: University of Chicago Press.

––– (1960) The Religion of Java. New York: Free Press.

GELLNER, E. (1969) "The great patron: a reinterpretation of tribal rebellions," Archives Européens de Sociologie, Tome 10, No. 1.

GERMANI, G. (1969) "Stages of modernization," International Journal, Vol. 24, No. 3 (Summer).

––– (1968) Politica y Sociedad in una Epoca de Transicion. Buenos Aires: Paidos.

GOBRON, G. (1949) History and Philosophy and Caodaism." Paris: Dervy.

GOLAY, F. H. (1961) The Philippines: Public Policy and National Economic Development. Ithaca: Cornell University Press.

––– (1969) et al (eds.) Underdevelopment and Economic Nationalism in Southeast Asia. Ithaca: Cornell University Press.

GONZALEZ-CASANOVA, P. (1965) "L'évolution de systéme des classes au Mexique, Cahiers Internationaux de Sociologie, Vol. 34.

GRACIARENA, J. (1968) Poder y Sociales en el Desarollo de América Latina. Buenos Aires: Paidos.

GROSLIER, G. (1921) Recherches sur les Cambodgiens. Paris: A. Challamel.

GROSSHOLTZ, J. (1964) Politics in the Philippines. Boston and Toronot: Little Brown.

GUERRERO, M. C. (1967) "The Colorum uprising, 1924-1931," Asian Studies, Vol. 5.

GULLICK, J. M. (1958) Indigenous Political Systems of Western Malaya. London: University of London, Athlone Press.

GUSFIELD, J. R. (1968) (ed.) "Tradition and modernity: conflict and congruence," Journal of Social Issues, Vol. 24. No. 4 (October).

GUSFIELD, J. R. (1966) "Tradition and modernity: misplaced polarities in the study of social change," American Journal of Society, Vol. 72 (January).

HAHHA, S. A., G. H. GARDNER (1969) (eds.) Arab Socialism. Leiden: Brill.

HANESSIAN, J., Jr. "Iranian land reforms," A.U.F.S., Vol. 12, No. 10.

HANKS, L. M., Jr. (1962) "Merit and power in the Thai social order," American Anthropologist, Vol. 64, No. 6 (December).

HANNA, W. A., "Modes of modernization in Southeast Asia," A.U.F.S., Vol. 17, No.

––– "The Indonesia crisis: early 1963 phase," A.U.F.S., Vol. 11, No. 8.

––– "Re-reviving a revolution," A.U.F.S., Vol. 11, No. 4.

––– "The Indonesia crisis: mid-1964 phase," A.U.F.S., Vol. 3, No. 7.

HAUSER, P. M. (1962) (ed.) Urbanization in Asia and the Far East. Paris: UNESCO.

––– (1960) (ed.) Urbanization in the Far East. Paris: UNESCO.

HARRISON, J. P. (1969) The Communists and Chinese Peasant Rebellions. New York: Atheneum.

HEATH, D. B., R. N. ADAMS (1965) (eds.) Contemporary Cultures and Societies in Latin America. New York: Random House.

HEINE-GELDERN, R. (1956) "Conception of state and kinship in Southeast Asia," Southeast Asian Program Data Paper No. 18: 1-13. Ithaca: Cornell University (April).

HENNESSY, C. A. M. "Shifting forces in the Bolivian revolution," The World Today, Vol. 20. No. 5.

HILLS, F. (1971) "Millenarian machines in South Vietnam," Comparative Studies in Society and History, Vol. 13, No. 3 (July).

HORTON, A. W. "Syrian stability and the Baath," A.U.F.S., Vol. 24, No. 1.

HOSELITZ, B. F. (1960) Sociological Aspects of Economic Growth. New York: Free Press.

HUIZER, G. (1968-1969) "Peasant organization in the process of agrarian reform in Mexico," Studies in Comparative International Development, Vol. 4, No. 6.

HUNTINGTON, S. P. (1965) "Political development and political decay," World Politics, Vol. 17, No. 3 (April).

――― , A. INKELES (eds.) Stability and Social Change. Boston: Little Brown.

――― (1962) "Values and social change in modern Japan," Asian Cultural Studies. No. 3 (October), Tokyo: International Christian University.

――― (1957) Tokugawa Religion. New York: Free Press.

――― (1965) "Japan's Cultural Identity," Journal of Asian Studies, Vol. 24, No. 24 (August). Jackson (ed.) Sociological Studies, Vol. 1. Cambridge: Cambridge University Press.

JACOBY, E. H. (1961) Agrarian Unrest in Southeast Asia. New York: Asia Publishing House.

JANSEN, M. B. (1965) (ed.) Changing Japanese Attitudes Toward Modernization. Princeton: Princeton University Press.

JUPP, J. (1968) "Constitutional developments in Ceylon since Independence," Pacific Affairs, Vol. 41. Reply, Vol. 43 (1970).

KAHIN, G. M. (1962) Nationalism and Revolution in Indonesia. Ithaca: Cornell University Press.

KATZ, D., R. L. KAHN, (1966) The Social Psychology of Organization. New York: Wiley.

KEES, H. (1933) "Agyten," in Handbuch der Altertumseissenschaft, Vol. 3, No. 1. Munich: Beck.

KEMAL SIDDIQUE (1970) "Political development in Indonesia, 1951-1957: an evaluation of S. N. Eisenstadt's 'Breakdown of Modernization'," Master Social Science thesis, University of Singapore.

KHALID bin SAYEED (1959) "Collapse of parliamentary democracy in Pakistan," The Middle East Journal, Vol. 12, No. 4 (Autumn).

KISHIMOTO, H. (1963) "Modernizatin versus westernization in the East," Cahiers d'Histoire Mondiale, 12.

KOTHARI, R. (1969) Politics in India. Boston: Little Brown.

KRADER, L. "Principles and structures in the organization of the Asiatic steppe-pastorialists," in Eisenstadt (ed.) Political Sociology.

KROFTA, K. (1936) "Bohemia to the extinction of the Premyslids" and "Bohemia in the fourteenth century" in Cambridge Medieval History, Vols. 6 and 7. Cambridge: Cambridge University Press.

LACOSTE, Y. (1966) Ibn Khaldoun, naissance de l'histoire, passé du tiers monde. Paris: Librairie François Maspero.

LANDSBERGER, H. A. (1969) (ed.) Latin American Peasant Movements. Ithaca: Cornell University Press.

LAROUI, A. (1970) L'histoire du Mahgreb. Paris: Librairie François Maspero.

LEACH, E. R. (1964, 1967) Political Systems of Highland Burma. London: London School of Economics. Boston: Beacon Press.

——— (1960) "The frontiers of Burma," Comparative Studies in Society and History, Vol. 3, No. 1.

LEGGE, J. D. (1964) Indonesia. Englewood Cliffs: Prentice Hall.

LEHMANN, D. (1971) "Political incorporation versus political stability: the case of Chilean agrarian reform, 1965-1970," Journal of Development Studies, Vol. 1, No. 4.

LERNER, D. (1958) The Passing of Traditional Society. New York: Free Press.

LEVY, M. (1966) Modernization and the Structure of Societies. Princeton: Princeton University Press.

LEWIS, J. W. (1970) (ed.) Party Leadership and Revolutionary Power in China. Cambridge: Cambridge University Press.

LIDDLE, R. W. (1970) Ethnicity, Party and National Integration. New Haven: Yale University Press.

LIJPHART, A. (1968) The Politics of Accommodation: Pluralism and Democracy in the Netherlands. Berkeley: University of California Press.

LINGAT, R. (1958) "La double crise de l'église Bouddique au Siam, 1767-1851," Journal of World History, Vol. 4, No. 2.

LIPSET, S. M., A. SOLARI (1967) (eds.) Elites in Latin America. New York: Oxford University Press.

LOPEZ, J. (1965) "Etude de quelque changements fondamentaux dans la politique et la société Brésilienne," Sociologie du Travail, No. 7.

LOUVET, S. (1883) Le Royaume de Cambodge. Paris: Leroux. (Published under the name of Jean Moura).

MACKIE, J. A. C. (1967) Problems of the Indonesian Inflation. Ithaca: Southeast Asia Program, Department of Asian Studies, Cornell University.

MADDOX, J. G. (1957) "Mexican land reform," New York: A.U.F.S. (A.U.F.S., JGH 5 57).

MAJID KHADLURI (1948) "The coup d'etat of 1936," Middle East Journal Vol. 2.

MA KYAN (1961) "King Mindon's councillors," Journal of the Burma Research Society, Vol. 44, No. 1.

MATZ, A. J. D. "The dynamics of change in Latin America," Journal of Inter-American Studies, Vol. 11, No. 1 (January).

MAZRUI, A. A. (1968) "From social Darwinism to current theories of modernization," World Politics, Vol. 21, No. 1 (October).

McALISTER, J., P. MUS, (1970) The Vietnamese and Their Revolution. New York: Center for International Studies, Princeton University.

McGEE, T. G. (1967) The Southeast Asian City. New York: Praeger.

MEED, C. K. (1964) Land Law and Custom in the Colonies. London: Oxford University Press.

MEILINK-ROELOFSZ, M. A. P. (1962) Asian Trade and European Influence in the Indonesian Archipelago between 1500 and about 1630. The Hague: Martinus Nijhoff.

MELLENA, R. L. (1961) "The basic democracies system in Pakistan," Asian Survey, Vol. 1, No. 6 (August).

MEYER, C. (1965) "Les mysterieuses relations entre le Roi du Cambodge et les 'patao' des jarai," Etudes Cambodgiennes, Vol. 4 (October-December).

MILLER, J. W. G. (1968) Education in Southeast Asia. Sydney: Ian Novak.

MILNE, R. S. (1969) "Political modernization in Malaysia," Journal of Commonwealth Political Studies, Vol. 7, No. 1 (March).

MILTON, R. N. (1965) "The basic Malay house," Journal of the Royal Asiatic Society, Malay branch, Vol. 24, No. 3.

MI MI KHAING (1947) Burmese Family. Bombay: Longmans, Green.

MOORE, C. (1970) Politics of North Africa. Boston: Little Brown.

MORELY, S. G. (1956) The Ancient Maya. Stanford: Stanford University Press.

MOSHE LISSAK (1969-1970) "Center and periphery in developing countries and prototypes of military elites," Studies in Comparative international development, Vol. 5, No. 7.

MURDOCK, G. P. (1960) (ed.) Social Structure in Southeast Asia. Chicago: Quadrangle.

MURPHY, R. F. (1971) The Dialection of Social Life. New York: Basic Books.

MUHAMMED SHAMUL HUG (1965) Education and Development Strategy in South and Southeast Asia. Honolulu: East-West Center Press.

NASH, M. (1965) The Golden Road to Modernity. New York: Wiley.

NAVARRO, M. G. (1965) "Mexico: the lop-sided revolution," in C. Veliz (ed.) Obstacles to Change in Latin America. London, New York: Oxford University Press.

PRINCE DHANI NIVAT (1955) "The reconstruction of King Rama 1 of the Chakri dynasty," Journal of the Siam Society, Vol. 43, No. 1.

NUMS, J. E. (1970-1971) "The new Latin American military coup," Studies in Comparative International Development, Vol. 6, No. 1.

OSBORNE, M. (1970) Region of Revolt: Focus on Southeast Asia. Sydney: Pergamon Press.

PAKEMAN, S. A. (1964) Ceylon. London: Been.

PALMIER, L. H. (1969) Social Status and Power in Java. Monographs on Social Anthropology; London: London School of Economics.

PALMIER, L. H. (1957) "Sukarno: the nationalist," Pacific Affairs, Vol. 30. No. 2 (July).

PARK, R. L. (1961) "Second thoughts on Asian democracy," Asian Survey, Vol. 1, No. 2 (April).

PATCH, R. W. "The last of Bolivia's MnR?," A.U.F.S., Vol. 11, No. 5.

––– "Bolivia's nationalism and the military," A.U.F.S., Vol. 16, No. 3.

––– "The Peruvian agrarian reform bill," A.U.F.S., Vol. 11, No. 3.

––– "A note on Bolivia and Peru," A.U.F.S., Vol. 9, No. 4.

––– "Peru's new president and agrarian reform," A.U.F.S., Vol. 10, No. 2.

––– "A note on Bolivia and Peru," A.U.F.S., Vol. 12. No. 2.

PAUKER, G. J. (1962) "Political doctrines and practical politics in Southeast Asia," Pacific Affairs, Vol. 35, No. 1 (Spring).

PEACOCK, J. (1968) Rites of Modernization: Symbols and Social Aspects of Indonesian Proletarian Drama. Chicago: University of Chicago Press.

PELLIOT, P. (1951) Mémoire sur les coutumes de Cambodge de Tcheon Takouan. Paris: Librairie d'Amerique et d'Orient.

PETRAS, J. "Revolution and guerilla movements in Latin America: Venezuela, Guatemala, Colombia, and Peru," in Petras and Zeitlin (eds.) Latin America: Reform or Revolution? Greenwich: Fawcett.

PHILIPS, H. (1965) Thai peasant personality. Berkeley: University of California Press.

PIERIS, R. (1956) Sinhalese Social Organization: The Kendya Period. Colombo: Ceylon University Press.

PLUVIER, J. M. (1965) Confrontations: A Study in Indonesian Politics. Kuala Lumpur: Oxford University Press.

POLANYI, K., C. M. ARENSBERG and H. W. PEARSON (1957) Trade and Market in Early Empires. New York: Free Press.

POMEROY, W. J. (1963) The Forest: A Personal Record of the Huk Guerilla Struggle in the Philippines. New York: International Publishers.

PRAPANCA, RAKAWI of MAJAPHIT (1960-1963) Java in the Fourteenth Century: A Study in Cultural History. The Hague: M. Nijhoff.

PURCELL, V. (1951) The Chinese in Southeast Asia. London, New York: Oxford University Press.

PUTHUCHEARY, J. J. (1960) Ownership and Control of the Malay Economy. Singapore: D. Moore for Eastern Universities Press.

QUIJANO, OBREGON A. (1968) "Tendencies in Peruvian development and class structure," in J. Petras and M. Zeitlin (eds.) Latin America: Reform or Revolution Greenwich: Fawcett.

RAIRBAIRN, G. (1968) Revolutionary Warfare and Communist Strategy. London: Faber.

RAMANATHAN, G. (1965) Educational Planning and National Integration. London: Asia Publishing House.

RATNAM, K. J. (1969) "Religion and politics in Malaya," in Tilman (ed.) Man, State and Society in Contemporary Southeast Asia. New York: Praeger.

——— (1965) Communalism and the Political Process in Malaya. Kuala Lumpur: University of Malaya Press.

REISCHAUER, E. O., J. K. FAIRBANK (1958) East Asia, The Great Tradition. Boston: Houghton Mifflin.

RIGGS, F. W. (1966) The Modernization of a Bureaucratic Polity. Honolulu: East-West Center Press.

——— (1964) Administration in Developing Countries. Boston: Houghton Mifflin.

——— (1959) "Agraria and industria: toward a typology of comparative administration," in W. J. Siffin (ed.) Toward a Comparative Study of Public Administration. Bloomington, Ind: Indiana University Press.

RIVLIN, B., J. S. Szyliowicz (eds.) The Contemporary Middle East: Traditions and Innovation. New York: Random House.

ROSE, S. (1968) "Political modernization in Asia," France-Asie/Asia, Vol. 22, No. 1 (First quarter).

ROSE' S. (1963) Politics in Southern Asia. London: Macmillan. New York: St. Martin's Press.

——— (1959) Socialism in Southern Asia. London, New York: Oxford University Press.

ROTH, G. (1968) "Personal rulership, patrimonialism and empire-building in the new state," World Politics, Vol. 20, No. 2 (January).

ROWE, J. W. "Argentina's restless military," A.U.F.S., Vol. 11, No. 2.

——— "Argentina: an election retrospect," A.U.F.S., Vol. 11, No. 1.

——— "Revolution or counterrevolution in Brazil? Part 2: from 'black Friday' to the new reforms," A.U.F.S., Vol. 11, No. 5.

——— "The 'revolution' and the 'system': notes on Brazilian politics. Part 1: seeds of the system," A.U.F.S., Vol. 12, No. 3.

——— "The 'revolution' and the 'system': notes on Brazilian politics. Part 2: the 'system'–full flower and crisis," A.U.F.S., Vol. 12, No. 4.

––– "The 'revolution' and the 'system': notes on Brazilian politics. Part 3: the 'revolution'–generals and technocrats," A.U.F.S., Vol. 12, No. 5.

RUSTOW, D. A. (1967) A World of Nations. Washington D.C.: Brookings Institution.

–––, ROBERT E. WARD (eds.) (1964) Political Modernization in Japan and Turkey. Princeton: Princeton University Press.

RYAN, B. (1953) Caste in Modern Ceylon. New Brunswick: Rutgers University Press.

––– (1952) "The Ceylonese villages and the new value system," Rural Sociology, Vol. 27, No. 4.

SANDERS, W. T. (1956) "The Central Mexican symbiotic region: a study in prehistoric settlement patterns," in G. R. Wilby (ed.) Prehistoric Settlement Patterns in the New World. New York: Viking Fund Publications in Anthropoligy, No. 23.

SAMIRE AMIN (1970) The Mahgreb in the Modern World, Hammondsworth: Penguin.

SARFATTI, M., A.E. BERGMAN (1969) Social Stratification in Peru. Politics and Modernization Series, No. 5. Berkeley: Institute of International Studies, University of California.

SARKISYANZ, E. (1965) Budhist Backgrounds of the Burmese Revolution. The Hague: Martinus Nijhoff.

SARTONO KARTODIRIDJO (1966) The Peasants' Revolt of Banten in 1888, Its Conditions, Course and Sequel: A Case Study of Social Movements in Indonesia. The Hague: M. Nijhoff.

SCHAPIRO, L. (1969) "Reflections on the changing role of the party in totalitarian polity," Studies in Comparative Communism, Vol. 2, No. 2 (April).

SCHILLING, W. (1970) "Der Sukarno und die 'neue ordnung' in Indonesien," Politische Studien, 21 Jahrgang (March-April).

SCHMIDT, H. (1963) "Postcolonial policies: a suggested interpretation of the Indonesian experience," Australian Journal of Politics and History, Vol. 9, No. 2 (November).

SCHMITTER, P. C. (1971) Interest, Conflict and Political Change in Brazil. Stanford: Stanford University Press.

SCHRIEKE, B. "Ruler and realm in early Java," in Schrieke Indonesian Sociological Studies, Part 2. The Hague, Bandung: Van Hoeve.

––– (1955) "The causes and effects of communism of the west coast of Sumatra," in Schrieke Indonesian Sociological Studies, Part 1, The Hague, Bandung: Van Hoeve.

SCIGLIANO, R. C. (1960) "The electoral process in South Vietnam: politics in an underdeveloped state," Midwest Journal of Political Science, Vol. 4, No. 2.

SCOTT, R. (1970) The Politics of the New State. London: Allen & Unwin.

SEGAL, R. "The new Egypt," Jerusalem Post, May 7, 1971.

SIFFIN, W. J. (1966) The Thai Bureaucracy. Honolulu: East-West Center Press.

SHARP, L. (1946) "Colonial regimes in Southeast Asia," Far Eastern Survey, Vol. 15.

SILCOCK, T. H. (1961) (ed.) Readings in Malayan Economics. Singapore: D. Moore for Eastern Universities Press.

SILVERT, K. (1969) "Latin America and its alternative future," International Journal, Vol. 24, No. 3 (Summer).

––– (1962) The Conflict Society, Reaction and Revolution in Latin America. New Orleans: Hauser.

SILVERT, K. H. "A note on Chile and Argentina," A.U.F.S., Vol. 8, No. 8.

SMITH, D. E. (1970) Religion and Political Development. Boston: Little Brown.

––– (1966) South Asian Politics and Religion. Princeton: Princeton University Press.

––– (1965) Religion and Politics in Burma. Princeton: Princeton University Press.

SOEDJATMOKO (1968) Economic Development as a Cultural Problem. Ithaca: Southeast Asia Program, Department of Asian Studies, Cornell University.

——— (1956) "The rise of political parties in Indonesia," in P. W. Thayer (ed.) Nationalism and Progress in Free Asia. Baltimore: Johns Hopkins Press.

SOEMARSAID MOERTONO (1968) State and Statecraft in Old Java: A Study of the Later Mataram Period, Sixteenth to Nineteenth Century. Ithaca: Modern Indonesia Project, Southeast Asia Program, Department of Asian Studies, Cornell University.

SOLOMON, R. L. (1969) "Saya San and the Burmese rebellion," Modern Asian Studies, Vol. 3, No. 3.

SORENSON, J. L. (1969) "The social bases of instability in Southeast Asia," Asian Survey, Vol. 9, No. 7 (July).

SPULER, B. (1960) The Muslim World. Leiden: Brill.

STARNER, F. L. (1961) Magsaysay and the Philippine Peasantry: The Agrarian Impact on Philippine Politics, 1953-1956. Berkeley: University of California Press.

STEINBERG, D. J. (1971) (ed.) In Search of Southeast Asia. New York: Praeger.

SUNKEL, O. "Change and frustration in Chile," in Veliz (ed.) op. cit.

SUTTON, F. X. (1963) "Social theory and comparative politics," in H. Eckstein and D. Apter (eds.) Comparative Politics: A Reader. New York: Free Press.

SWANSON, E. (1969) Rules of Descent. Studies in the Sociology of Parentage. Ann Arbor. Anthropological Papers, Museum of Anthropology, University of Michigan

TANHAM, G. K. (1967) Communist Revolutionary Warfare. New York: Praeger.

THAUNG (1959) "Burmese kingship in theory and practice and the reign of King Mindon," Journal of the Burma Research Society, Vol. 42, No. 2.

THEIRRY, S. (1959) "La personne sacrée de Roi dans la littérature populaire Cambodgienne," Studies in the History of Religions, Vol. 4.

TILMAN, R. O. (1969) (ed.) Man, State and Society in Contemporary Southeast Asia New York: Praeger.

———(1964) Bureaucratic Transition in Malaya. Durham: Duke University Press.

——— (1963) "The bureaucratic legacy of modern Malaya," Indian Journal of Public Administration, Vol. 9, No. 2 (April-June).

TINKER, H. (1964) "The city in the Asian polity," in Tinker Ballot Box and Bayone London, New York: Oxford University Press.

TOURAINE, A., D. PECAUT (1967-1968) "Working class consciousness and econom development," Studies in Comparative International Development, Vol. 3, No. 4.

——— (1965) "Social mobility, class relations, and nationalism in Latin America," Studies in Comparative International Devleopment, Vol. 1.

TRAGER, F. N. (1959) (ed.) Marxism in Southeast Asia. Stanford: Stanford University Press.

——— (1959) "Political divorce in Burma," Foreign Affairs, Vol. 37, No. 2 (January).

TURNER, Y. (1971) (ed.) Colonisation in Africa, 1870-1960. Cambridge: Cambridge University Press.

United Nations Report (n.d.) "Changing socioeconomic patterns in the Middle East" 299-213.

VAN der KROEF, J. (1959) "Javanese messianic expectations: their origin and cultural context," Comparative Studies in Society and History, Vol. 1.

VAN LEAR, J. C. (1955) Indonesian Trade and Society. The Hague, Bandung: Van Hoeve.

VELOSO, ABUEVA J. (1970) "Administrative culture and behavior and middle civil servants in the Philippines," in E. W. Weidner (ed.) Development Administration in Asia. Durham: Duke University Press.

VERNADSKII, G. (1938) "The scope and contents of Genghis Khan's yasa," Harvard Journal of Asiatic Studies, Vol. 3.

VINOGRADOV, A., J. WATERBURY (1971) "Situations of contested legitimacy in Morocco: an alternative framework," Comparative Studies in Society and History, Vol. 13, No. 1 (January).

VITTACHI, T. (1967) The Fall of Sukarno. New York: Praeger.

WALES, H. G. Q. (1934) Ancient Siamese Government and Administration. London: B. Quaritch.

WALLERSTEIN, I. M. (1960) Social Change, The Colonial Situation. New York: Wiley.

WANG GUNGWU (1964) (ed.) Malaysia. New York: Praeger.

WARRINER, D. (1969) Land Reform in Principle and Practice. Oxford: Clarendon Press.

WATERBURY, J. (1970) The Commander of the Faithful: The Moroccan Elite. London: Weidenfeld & Nicholson.

WEAVER, J. L. (1969-1970) "Political styles of the Guatemalan military elite," Studies in Comparative International Development, Vol. 5, No. 4.

WEBER, M. (1947) "Gerontocracy, patriarchalism and patrimonial authority," in M. Weber The Theory of Social and Economic Organization (ed.) T. Parsons. New York: Oxford University Press.

WELLS, K. (1939) Thai Buddhism: Its Rites and Activities. Bangkok: Bangkok Times Press.

WERTHEIM, W. F. "Southeast Asia," International Encyclopedia of the Social Sciences. Vol. 1.

WHEATLEY, P. (1971) The Piovot of Four Quarters. Edinburgh: Edinburgh University Press.

––– (1969) City as Symbol. London: H. K. Lewis.

WHITAKER, C. S. Jr, (1967) "A dysrythmic process of political change," World Politics, Vol. 19, No. 2 (January).

WHITMORE, J. K. (1970) Vietnamese Adaptations of Chinese Government Structure in the Fifteenth Century. New Haven: Southeast Asian Studies, Yale University.

WINSTEDT, R. O. (1947) "Kinship and enthronement in Malaya," Journal of the Royal Asiatic Society, Malay Branch, Vol. 20, Part 1 (June).

WOLTERS, O. W.(1967) Early Indonesian Commerce. Ithaca: Cornell University Press.

WOODSIDE, A. (1970) Vietnam and the Chinese Model. Cambridge: Harvard University Press.

WOODWARD, C. A. (1969) The Growth of a Party System in Ceylon. Providence: Brown University Press.

WORCESTER, D. E. (1969) "The Spanish-American past, enemy of change," Journal of Inter-American Studies, Vol. 11, No. 1 (January).

WRIGGINS, W. H. (1960) Ceylon: Dilemmas of a New Nation. Princeton: Princeton University Press.

WYATT, D. K. (1968) "Family politics in nineteenth century Thailand," Journal of Southeast Asian History, Vol. 9, No. 2.

YI YI (1961) "The judicial system of King Mindon," Journal of the Burma Research Society, Vol. 44, No. 2.

ZEITLIN, M., J. PETRAS (1970) "The working class vote in Chile: Christan democracy versus Marxist," British Journal of Socialism, Vol. 21, No. 1 (March).

ZOLBERG, A. R. (1969) Creating Political Order: The Party States of West Africa. Chicago: Rand McNally.

S. N. EISENSTADT is Professor of Sociology at the Hebrew University in Jerusalem. He has been Visiting Professor at Harvard, M.I.T., Chicago and other universities. He recently spent a semester as Fellow at the Netherlands Institute for Advanced Study in the Humanities and Social Sciences. Dr. Eisenstadt has also spent a year as a Fellow at the Center for Advanced Study in the Social and Behavioral Sciences (Palo Alto). He is the author of several major works in the field of comparative political development and the overall area of political sociology, including: The Political Systems of Empires *(winner of the MacIver Award for 1963);* Modernization: Protest and Change; From Generation to Generation; Social Differentiation and Social Stratification; The Absorption of Immigrants; Israeli Society; The Protestant Ethic and Modernization; *and the forthcoming* Tradition, Change and Modernity. *He has also edited a number of important collections of contributions to comparative analysis, such as:* The Decline of Empires; Political Sociology *(a reader); and (with Stein Rokkan)* Building States and Nations: Models, Analyses and Data Across Three Worlds. *Professor Eisenstadt is a Member of the Israel Academy of Science and Humanities; an Honary Foreign Member of the American Academy of Arts and Sciences; and a Foreign Member of the American Philosophical Society.*

A Better Way of Getting New Information

esearch, survey and policy studies that say what needs to be said— more, no less.

he Sage Papers Program

ve regularly-issued original paperback series that bring, at an unusually w cost, the timely writings and findings of the international scholarly mmunity. Since the material is updated on a continuing basis, each ries rapidly becomes a unique repository of vital information.

uthoritative, and frequently seminal, works that NEED to be available

- To scholars and practitioners
- In university and institutional libraries
- In departmental collections
- For classroom adoption

age Professional Papers

OMPARATIVE POLITICS SERIES
ITERNATIONAL STUDIES SERIES
DMINISTRATIVE AND POLICY STUDIES SERIES
MERICAN POLITICS SERIES

age Policy Papers

HE WASHINGTON PAPERS

SAGE PUBLICATIONS
The Publishers of Professional Social Science
Beverly Hills • London

VOLUME 1 (1970)

01-001 **J.Z. Namenwirth & H. D. Lasswell,** The changing language of American values: a computer study of selected party platforms $2.50/£1.05

01-002 **K. Janda,** A conceptual framework for the comparative analysis of political parties $1.90/£.80

01-003 **K. Thompson,** Cross-national voting behavior research $1.50/£.60

01-004 **W. B. Quandt,** The comparative study of political elites $2.00/£.85

01-005 **M. C. Hudson,** Conditions of political violence and instability $1.90/£.80

01-006 **E. Ozbudun,** Party cohesion in western democracies $3.00/£1.30

01-007 **J. R. Nellis,** A model of developmental ideology in Africa $1.40/£.55

01-008 **A. Kornberg, et al.,** Semi-careers in political organizations $1.40/£.55

01-009 **F. I. Greenstein & S. Tarrow,** Political orientations of children $2.90/£1.25

01-010 **F. W. Riggs,** Administrative reform and political responsiveness: a theory of dynamic balance $1.50/£.60

01-011 **R. H. Donaldson & D. J. Waller,** Stasis and change in revolutionary elites: a comparative analysis of the 1956 Central Party Committees in China and the USSR $1.90/£.80

01-012 **R. A. Pride,** Origins of democracy: a cross-national study of mobilization, party systems and democratic stability $2.90/£1.25

VOLUME II (1971)

01-013 **S. Verba, et al.,** The modes of democratic participation $2.80/£1.20

01-014 **W. R. Schonfeld,** Youth and authority in France $2.80/£1.20

01-015 **S. J. Bodenheimer,** The ideology of developmentalism $2.40/£1.00

01-016 **L. Sigelman,** Modernization and the political system $2.50/£1.05

01-017 **H. Eckstein,** The evaluation of political performance: problems and dimensions $2.90/£1.25

01-018 **T. Gurr & M. McLelland,** Political performance: a twelve nation study $2.90/£1.25

01-019 **R. F. Moy,** A computer simulation of democratic political development $2.70/£1.15

01-020 **T. Nardin,** Violence and the state $2.70/£1.15

01-021 **W. Ilchman,** Comparative public administration and "conventional wisdom" $2.40/£1.00

01-022 **G. Bertsch,** Nation-building in Yugoslavia $2.25/£.95

01-023 **R. J. Willey,** Democracy in West German trade unions $2.40/£1.00

01-024 **R. Rogowski & L. Wasserspring,** Does political development exist Corporatism in old and new societies $2.40/£1.00

VOLUME III (1972)

01-025 **W. T. Daly,** The revolutionary $2.10/£.90

01-026 **C. Stone,** Stratification and polit cal change in Trinidad and Jamai $2.10/£.90

01-027 **Z. Y. Gitelman,** The diffusion of political innovation: from Easter Europe to the Soviet Union $2.50/£1.05

01-028 **D. P. Conradt,** The West German party system $2.40/£1.00

01-029 **J. R. Scarritt,** Political developm and culture change theory [Afric $2.50/£1.05

01-030 **M. D. Hayes,** Policy outputs in th Brazilian states $2.25/£.95

01-031 **B. Stallings,** Economic dependen in Africa and Latin America $2.50/£1.05

01-032 **J. T. Campos & J. F. McCamant,** Cleavage shift in Colombia: analy sis of the 1970 elections $2.90/£

01-033 **G. Field & J. Higley,** Elites in developed societies [Norway] $2.25/£.95

01-034 **J. S. Szyliowicz,** A political analy sis of student activism [Turkey] $2.80/£1.20

01-035 **E. C. Hargrove,** Professional role in society and government [Engl $2.90/£1.25

01-036 **A. J. Sofranko & R. J. Bealer,** Unbalanced modernization and domestic instability $2.90/£1.2

VOLUME IV (1973)

01-037 **W. A. Cornelius,** Political learnin among the migrant poor $2.90/

01-038 **J. W. White,** Political implication cityward migration [Japan] $2.50/£1.05

01-039 **R. B. Stauffer,** Nation-building i global economy: the role of the multi-national corporation $2.25/£.95

01-040 **A. Martin,** The politics of econo policy in the U.S. $2.50/£1.05

Forthcoming, summer/fall 1973

01-041 **M. B. Welfling,** Political Instituti alization [African party systems $2.70*/£1.15

01-042 **B. Ames,** Rhetoric and reality in militarized regime [Brazil] $2.40*/£1.00

01-043 **E. C. Browne,** Coalition theories $2.90*/£1.25

01-044 **M. Barrera,** Information and ideology: a study of Arturo Frondizi $2.40*/£1.00

*denotes tentative pri

Papers 01-045 through 01-048 to be annou

International Studies

Vincent Davis *and* Maurice East, *University of Kentucky.*

ME I (1972)

E. E. Azar, et al., International
events interaction analysis
$2.80/£1.20

J. H. Sigler, et al., Applications of
events data analysis $3.00/£1.30

J. C. Burt, Decision networks and
the world population explosion
$2.25/£.95

J. A. Caporaso, Functionalism and
regional integration $2.90/£1.25

E. R. Wittkopf, Western bilateral
aid allocations $2.50/£1.05

T. L. Brewer, Foreign policy situations: American elite responses to
variations in threat, time, and
surprise $2.50/£1.05

W. F. Weiker, Decentralizing government in modernizing nations
[Turkish provinces] $2.70/£1.15

F. A. Beer, The political economy
of alliances: benefits, costs, and
institutions in NATO $2.10/£.90

C. Mesa-Lago. The labor force,
employment, unemployment, and
underemployment in Cuba: 1899-
1970 $2.70/£1.15

P. M. Burgess & R. W. Lawton, Indi-
cators of international behavior:
an assessment of events data
research $3.00/£1.30

W. Minter, Imperial network and
external dependency [Angola]
$2.70/£1.15

02-012   J. R. Redick, Military potential of
Latin American nuclear energy
programs $2.40/£1.00

VOLUME II (1973)

02-013   B. H. Steiner, Arms races, diplo-
macy, and recurring behavior
$2.10/£.90

02-014   C. W. Kegley, Jr., A general
empirical typology of foreign
policy behavior $2.80/£1.20

02-015   G. T. Hilton, A review of the
dimensionality of nations project
$2.80/£1.20

02-016   E. Weisband, The ideology of
American foreign policy
$2.70/£1.15

Forthcoming

02-017   B. Abrahamsson & J. L. Steckler,
The strategic aspects of seaborne
oil $2.50*/£1.05

02-018   D. Mookerjee & R. L. Morrill,
Urbanization in a developing
economy [India] $2.80*/£1.20

02-019   R. J. Art, The influence of foreign
policy on seapower: new weapons
and weltpolitik in Wilhelminian
Germany $2.40*/£1.00

02-020   D. Druckman, Human factors in
international relations $2.90*/£1.25

*denotes tentative prices

Papers 02-021 through 02-024 to be announced.

Professional Papers in

ministrative and Policy Studies

H. George Frederickson, *Indiana University.*

ME I (1973)

E. Ostrom, W. Baugh, R. Guarasci,
R. Parks, G. Whitaker. Community
organization and the provision of
police services $3.00/£1.30

R. S. Ahlbrandt, Jr., Municipal fire
protection services $2.70/£1.15

D. O. Porter with D. C. Warner,
T. W. Porter. The politics of budget-
ing federal aid [local school districts]
$3.00/£1.30

J. P. Viteritti, Police, politics and
pluralism in New York City
$2.70/£1.15

73 summer/fall papers will include—
R. L. Schott, Professionals in public
service: characteristics and education of engineer federal executives

03-006   C. Argyris, On organizations of the
future

03-007   O. White, Jr., Psychic energy and
organizational change

03-008   D. C. Perry & P.A. Sornoff, Politics
at the street level: police administration and the community

03-009   H. Margolis, Technical advice on
policy issues

03-010   M. Holden, Jr., The politics of poor
relief: a study in ambiguities

03-011   S. S. Nagel, Minimizing costs and
maximizing benefits in providing
legal services to the poor

03-012   Yong Hyo Cho & H. George
Frederickson, Determinants of
public policy in the American
States: a model for synthesis